READY-TO-GO

Writing Lessons

That Teach Key Strategies

by Patricia Tabb and Nancy Delano Moore

S
P

New York •   dney
Mexic

Dedication

To our teachers, Miss Mary Belle Smith and Pauline Efford Delano, and to all teachers who inspire their students to keep writing.

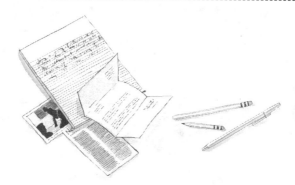

Acknowledgments

Thanks to the Centurion Team of Winburn Middle School in Lexington, Kentucky, especially teachers Robin Black and Sara Delano Moore and students Catherine Allen, Jimmy Crouch, Allison Crutcher, Laura Grabau, Michelle Grise, Chris Kirchner, Seth Kirk, Ryan Lang, Benjamin Lawler, Caitlin Milligan, Kelsey Minarik, Sarah Schaefer, Anthony Schmidt, Jillian Wang, and Lucas Wilcox. They're winning writers.

Nathaniel Hein Delano offered fine suggestions on middle school lessons, and Will Citrin carried out a helpful review of our manuscript.

Sarah Longhi generously provided editorial support and expertise.

Our families gave unending support and encouragement. We thank Hullie, Sara, Frank, Amy, Austin, and Kiernan; Randy, Ashley, and Anne Randolph; ACE and Tabby Simpkin.

"Sparky" by Earl Nightengale. Cited in *Chicken Soup for the Teenage Soul*, Jack Canfield, et. al, ed. Scholastic Inc., 1997.

"Subway Rush Hour" from *Collected Poems* by Langston Hughes. Copyright © 1994 by the Estate of Langston Hughes. Reprinted by permission of Alfred A.Knopf, a Division of Random House Inc.

"The Thought Fox" from *Selected Poems 1957–1967* by Ted Hughes. Copyright © 1957 by Ted Hughes. Originally appeared in *The New Yorker*. Reprinted by permission of HarperCollins Publishers Inc. Also by Faber & Faber, 3 Queen Square, London-WC1N 3AU England.

Cover design by Norma Ortiz
Interior design by Sydney Wright
Interior illustrations by Brian Floca

ISBN 0-439-13847-7

Contents

Introduction

Dear Fellow Teachers,

You're holding in your hands the book about writing we needed when we were students in the middle school grades years ago. We loved to write, but we needed to learn the essential skills and strategies required for good writing. *Ready-to-Go Writing Lessons That Teach Key Strategies* goes beyond teaching the writing basics. It provides practical lesson plans and helpful tips for teachers, relevant activities for students, and valuable resources for learning the art of writing.

The skills and strategies targeted in these lessons—now required by most states in their language arts standards—are connected to important writing outcomes. With this book, students can master these objectives and satisfy many language arts requirements. See "How to Use This Book" (page 6) for more information on the application of these lessons and the standards.

We believe that the purpose of writing instruction in middle school is to help students shape their thoughts on the page. We are convinced that students have a storehouse of writing material to share even though they may not know it. We also are convinced that students need strategies to help them tap into that writing material and develop their writing into meaningful outcomes.

Because we know that writing can be a solitary experience, we do not want young writers to feel alone on the blank page. This collection of lessons introduces your students to Soccer Sal, a friendly writing companion who offers advice and training in eighteen independent writing lessons, each emphasizing a different strategy or skill. This character uses student-developed samples and an engaging soccer analogy to help your students understand each lesson objective and, ultimately, become winners in the writing game.

In writing this book, we have worked hard to come to terms with putting the writing process on paper. We hope these lessons will remove some of the mystery and confusion surrounding how to write—and offer clearly defined skills, strategies, and goals that will help your young writers gain confidence in and develop an enthusiasm for their written work.

Patricia Tabb and Nancy Delano Moore

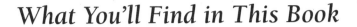

What You'll Find in This Book

Teacher planning pages with lesson plans that include the following:

✳ **Introduction** opens the lesson.

✳ **Focus** identifies the strategies or skills for that lesson.

✳ **Lesson activity** explains specific exercises and assignments you'll find on the reproducible lesson pages.

✳ **Writing links** lists related writing outcomes for the focus strategies or skills.

✳ **Introducing the lesson** presents an idea to help you capture student interest and orient students to the lesson's focus.

✳ **Literature resource** offers a useful, relevant excerpt from favorite young adult literature or an author's comments on his or her craft.

✳ **Tip** provides pointers culled from teacher experiences.

Reproducible student lesson pages with a special character, Soccer Sal, who uses a kid-friendly voice to guide students through the lessons, explanations, and exercises.

Listen Up introduces and explains the target strategy or skill and goal.

Practice presents Soccer Sal's example and an opportunity for students to practice the skill introduced.

Play the Game assigns a related independent writing activity.

✓ **Check It** encourages students to review and reflect on the writing in the activity.

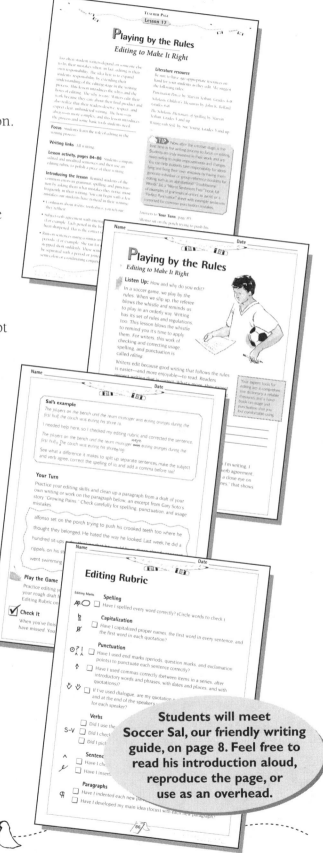

Students will meet Soccer Sal, our friendly writing guide, on page 8. Feel free to read his introduction aloud, reproduce the page, or use as an overhead.

Ready-to-Go Writing Lessons That Teach Key Strategies
Scholastic Professional Books

How to Use This Book

Adapt Lessons to Suit Your Students' Needs

Ready-to-Go Writing Lessons That Teach Key Strategies is organized for easy use. A table of contents helps you quickly locate the skill and goal for each lesson. Feel free to pick and choose the lessons according to your classroom needs. The lessons have a built-in flexibility:

✳ Each lesson can stand alone.

✳ Each lesson can combine with other lessons to form a classroom packet.

✳ The lessons can be used sequentially as a curriculum.

✳ The lessons can be used selectively across grade levels.

✳ The lessons can be used for advanced students.

✳ The lessons can be used as tutorials for students with specific skill needs.

✳ The lessons can be used individually as introductions to language arts curriculum.

Sections of the lessons can be used to introduce class assignments. For example, you can make use of the Listen Up and Practice sections of any lesson and substitute a teacher-selected writing assignment in place of Play the Game. Finally, general reference pages, such as revision and editing checklists (pages 74 and 86) and a skills and strategies checklist (pages 94–95), are key components of the book and will be helpful to you in planning for your classroom needs.

Make the Standards Connection

Ready-to-Go Writing Lessons That Teach Key Strategies focuses on essential writing objectives now found in state and national language arts standards. The lesson plans incorporate many of the same skills and outcomes contained in the standards. Here's a sampling that includes familiar labels for these strategies, skills, and outcomes:

Strategies and Skills

Freewriting to generate ideas	Editing	Writing the rough draft
Revising	Peer editing	Creating sentence variety
Peer revising	Organizing ideas	Developing one's writing voice
Reading to write	Writing for an audience	Evaluating one's writing

Possible Outcomes/Genre Connections

Personal narrative	Poem	Biography
Expository essay	Letter	Short story
Descriptive paragraph	Transactive writing	Reflective letter
Informative writing	Personal essay	Book review
Script	Persuasive essay	

Ready-to-Go Writing Lessons That Teach Key Strategies
Scholastic Professional Books

Before You Begin

Helping Students Understand Why They Write

We want students to find a purpose for writing. We want them to learn to think on the page, to discover what they already know, and to take time to express their ideas in new and effective ways. We want them to know that when they write, they manage their thoughts better because they take time to jot down ideas, to delete, to organize, to substitute words and sentences, to add new thoughts, and to reflect on their work. That sense of purpose gives meaning to all kinds of writing—from classroom assignments to childhood memoirs, short stories, or even letters to friends.

Students may enjoy hearing novelist Joan Didion's perspective on the purpose of writing. She says: "I write entirely to find out what's on my mind, what I'm thinking, what I'm looking at, what I'm seeing and what it means, what I want and what I'm afraid of" ("On Keeping a Notebook").

Helping Students Establish Good Writing Habits

Like a good coach, you'll want to employ strategies that help your students gain a sense of purpose when they write and develop good habits. Here are a few ideas:

✳ Teacher modeling: Write when your students write. You also can help your students by demonstrating good reading and writing strategies, such as using sensory details to compose a descriptive paragraph or adding new ideas to revise a rough draft. (The overhead projector and chart paper are excellent tools for whole-class or small-group demonstrations.)

✳ Teacher and peer feedback: Students thrive as writers when you regularly praise their writing and frequently use examples from student work to model good writing techniques. Just as a soccer coach trains players by teaching skills, overseeing practice, and identifying strengths and weak-nesses, you can urge young writers to hone their writing skills and develop a repertoire of strategies to bring with them to the blank page. Peers play an important role at this age, as well, and it's important to teach your students how to criticize constructively. As they practice writing and give and receive feedback, their writing voices grow stronger and they become better communicators, whether they are conveying information, supporting an opinion, telling a story, or sharing thoughts.

✳ Student journal or notebook: This tool provides students with a safe space to express themselves freely, collect topic ideas, and develop writing projects. This collecting and developing space is the answer to the frequent complaint, "I don't know what to write about!" In their journals or notebooks, students "plant" idea seeds that they can turn to for inspiration—and eventually make blossom and grow.

✳ Technology and publication: Allow frequent opportunities for students to use a word-processing program to publish their work. Young writers can compose anywhere, but computers provide the quickest and easiest means of making the writing look professional and important. Students who see their writing move from scribbles to a clean printed page see themselves as real writers.

Let the lessons begin!

Meet Soccer Sal

Hey! My name is Soccer Sal and I'm a star player. Not to brag, but I've been working hard on skills and moves in my writing the same way I've been practicing for my game on the soccer field. I've decided to share some of the best strategies and ideas with you. I can show you how writing with style is just like playing a great game of soccer.

The writing strategies I'll show you are my winning team when it comes to putting my ideas down on paper. And they can be yours, too. As you work on each page of a lesson from this book, I'll be there to guide you and cheer you on.

Here's how it goes:

In *Ready-to-Go Writing Lessons*, I kick off every lesson with a writing skill or strategy that will help you write better. By the time we've worked through the lesson, you'll get the hang of that skill or strategy.

When you read through each lesson, try these tips to help you stay focused:

1. Underline key words or phrases that remind you about the skill or strategy you're learning. Ask yourself, *What's the main point and how is this important in my writing?*

2. Know what to expect. Every lesson moves through the following four sections:

Listen Up introduces you to a new writing strategy or skill.

Practice provides a good example, and **Your Turn** gives you a chance to try it on your own.

Play the Game assigns an independent writing activity.

Check It helps you appreciate and think critically about the writing you've done.

Are you ready? Let's hit the field!

Ready-to-Go Writing Lessons That Teach Key Strategies
Scholastic Professional Books

The Familiar Field
Finding Writing Material

"But my life is boring!" That's most students' first complaint when we ask them to write about events from their lives. So how do we convince them that they can find real writing material in their ordinary days? We begin by introducing them to a writer whose ordinary days provided material for writing and encouraging them to look more carefully at their own lives for writing material.

Focus Students look in their own worlds for writing material.

Writing links Personal narrative, poetry, expository and/or persuasive essay, and drama.

Lesson activity, pages 11–13 Students list people, hobbies, memories, books, movies, passions, and experiences for writing material and then choose one to write about in a paragraph to include in a personal narrative.

Introducing the lesson Ask students what the word *material* means. Chances are, they'll tell you it's fabric, like a T-shirt or jeans or sweats. Ask them what it might mean in writing. Some of them may know that it's a collection of personal and direct experiences and all the emotions and ideas surrounding those experiences that a writer uses.

Literature resource Reading aloud Chapter Eight in Laura Ingalls Wilder's *Little House on the Prairie* allows students to hear an example of writing material inspired by the ordinary events in an individual's life. Call particular attention to the passage below where the author describes details of this everyday pioneer experience of helping Pa make a door in a way that makes the event real for the reader:

"I have no more nails, but I'll not keep on waiting til I can make a trip to Independence," he said. "A man doesn't need nails to build a house or make a door."

After breakfast he hitched up Pet and Patty, and taking his ax he went to get timber for the door. Laura helped wash the dishes and make the beds, but that day Mary minded the baby. Laura helped Pa make the door. Mary watched, but Laura handed him his tools.

With the saw he sawed logs the right length for a door. He sawed shorter lengths for cross-pieces. Then with the ax he split the logs into slabs, and smoothed them nicely. He laid the long slabs together on the ground and placed the shorter slabs across them. Then with the auger he bored holes through the cross-pieces into the long slabs. Into every hole he drove a wooden peg that fitted tightly.

That made the door. It was a good oak door, solid and strong.

Point out to students that this activity in prairie life is comparable to the description of baking a pan of brownies. In their way and time, both are ordinary activities. Once written, both accounts provide the writer's observations and particular perspective on an ordinary event.

You can extend this lesson to show students that the same material can be transformed into a completely different outcome or genre. For example, the

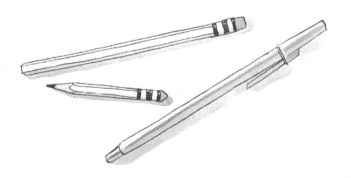

Ready-to-Go Writing Lessons That Teach Key Strategies
Scholastic Professional Books

narrative description of Pa's construction of the door can be rewritten as an informative essay on how to build a door without nails using pioneer techniques. Using their work from pages 12 and 13, encourage students to generate a list of topics in their lives, topics that they can call themselves "experts" on or topics they'd like to learn more about. When these lists are posted or kept in writing journals or notebooks, students will always have a source to return to for rich ideas.

Notes:

> **TIP** Students need to see teachers as writers, too. Share an experience from your early school days to reinforce the idea that the ordinary lives of the people they know are full of meaningful experiences and people. Later, read aloud a short written account of that experience to demonstrate the way writing grows out of these real events that we chat about—and care about. It's true, these everyday events provide rich material for writing.

The Familiar Field

Finding Writing Material

Listen Up: Where do you find your writing material?

My best material for writing comes from the people, emotions, ideas, and experiences in my everyday life. I find plenty of writing material on my own soccer field, so to speak. And you'll find the same. Let me explain.

Writing about my game means I can describe the game as I experienced it—play by play. My written words can show you what I observed, thought, and felt as a lanky, ponytailed player dribbled toward me, as I defended our goal, and later as I pushed the ball down the field, back and forth, between my feet. Even though I do play in an ordinary neighborhood on an ordinary team that doesn't make the headlines, the descriptions of the flat green field, the plays and players, and the frantic feelings are all mine, and that's what makes my writing worth the effort. Take it from me, what you know best and what you're most interested in will give you the best material for your writing.

Practice

Sometimes writers think they need a dramatic event before they can write. My pal Ben wrote about this in his freewriting at the beginning of the year.

Sal's example

I can't write and I can't remember anything to write about. I don't have any good inspirations, even though I like to read books. I don't know what to write about. I don't have anything real dramatic happening in my life.

Ben Lawler
Winburn Middle School

Sound familiar? Where can Ben find writing material? He can begin with his interest in reading books. That's an experience worth writing about. He also can pay attention to the ordinary events of his day—that familiar walk or ride to school, or waiting in line for the dreaded cafeteria grub—and write about them.

Ready-to-Go Writing Lessons That Teach Key Strategies
Scholastic Professional Books

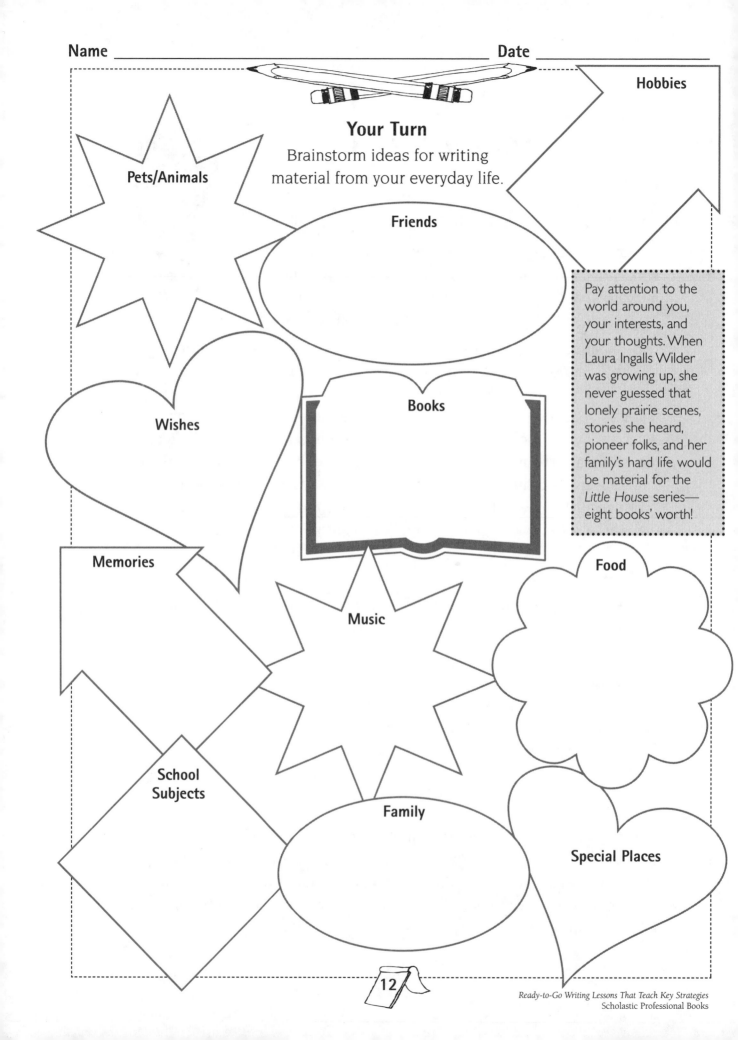

Your Turn
Brainstorm ideas for writing material from your everyday life.

Hobbies

Pets/Animals

Friends

Wishes

Books

Memories

Pay attention to the world around you, your interests, and your thoughts. When Laura Ingalls Wilder was growing up, she never guessed that lonely prairie scenes, stories she heard, pioneer folks, and her family's hard life would be material for the *Little House* series— eight books' worth!

Food

Music

School Subjects

Family

Special Places

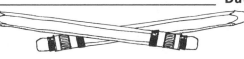

Play the Game

Choose one of your ideas from **Your Turn** and write a short account of an experience you've had involving that person, place, or thing.

My writing idea: _____

_____
(title)

_____

_____

_____

_____

_____

_____

_____

_____

_____   Use your expert
                                                   knowledge of your
_____   topic, add lots of details,
                                                   and write in complete
_____   sentences to make your
                                                   personal narrative as
_____   entertaining as possible.

_____

_____

_____

_____

_____

_____

_____

_____

 ## Check It

Reread your piece. Star new ideas to write about in the future.

Ready-to-Go Writing Lessons That Teach Key Strategies
Scholastic Professional Books

Kicking the Ball Around
Freewriting to Loosen Up

Just as stretching and running laps warm up the player for a game, freewriting prepares the writer to jump into the act of writing. When students have nothing to say or experience a writing block, freewriting can help them generate ideas or find direction. With an idea or direction in mind, writers can freewrite again to further develop their ideas. Freewriting also can loosen students' writing muscles when they are assigned a topic—it can take the edge off writing under pressure (especially for a standardized test). And the best part about freewriting is the "free" part—no concern about what's correct or proper.

Focus To provide students with a tool to jump-start and spur on their writing.

Writing links All writing.

Lesson activity, pages 15–17 Students practice freewriting, choose a direction, and then freewrite again for five minutes without stopping.

Introducing the lesson Present freewriting to students by modeling the process on an overhead projector. Encourage students to select a topic for you to model freewriting. You should write for a short time (two to five minutes) without pausing (of course, you'll write all you can, including "I need an idea" when you get stuck). Afterward, read your freewriting aloud and underline any ideas you can pursue. This modeling allows students to observe how words scribbled on the page freely and continuously can become writing ideas.

Then challenge students to freewrite to discover their own ideas and topics (set a two- to five-minute time period). Invite students to read through their freewriting and underline any exciting writing ideas. These ideas can become prompts for their practice freewriting on pages 16 and 17. Suggest that

students add variety to their prompts by including words, phrases, sentences, or even short paragraphs, such as the following: Trip; Bicycling in the park; Write about the time you were late; Suppose you were appointed head of the SPCA. You have limited funds but unlimited concern and energy. What would be your first project?

Students may have extra ideas and you may want to collect some of these in an "idea box" to create a grab bag of future writing topics. (A shoe box or large manila envelope can serve as your "idea box.")

Literature resource One writer explains how he frees up his flow of ideas: "I usually begin by freewriting; that is, I try to discover the focus by writing and seeing what comes out. I am looking for words, ideas, combinations that surprise me. . . . Essentially I babble on my computer screen" (Christopher Scanlan from Donald Murray's *The Craft of Revision*). We want to encourage that same freedom in students' writing, as in the student sample in the lesson.

> **TIP** Freewriting can be used on a regular basis (say, once a week) as a stamina builder. Over time, students will be able to sustain the flow of their ideas for increasingly longer periods of time. Start out with freewriting for two minutes and work up gradually. Students can keep track of how they're doing by counting the number of lines they've written each time and watching them increase. Some students may enjoy recording their progress on a personal chart in the writing notebook. They'll build more confidence as they discover how easy it is to fill a page with ideas—whether they're generating topic ideas or overcoming a writing block later in the process.

Ready-to-Go Writing Lessons That Teach Key Strategies
Scholastic Professional Books

Kicking the Ball

Freewriting to Loosen Up

Listen Up: What is freewriting and how does it help?

When I think of freewriting, I think of warm-up. In soccer, that's when I kick the ball around to prepare for the game. In writing, warm-up is when I scribble down lots of words, phrases, and sentences to see what writing ideas come to mind. I freewrite when I'm looking for a topic or looking for more to say on a topic. I write anything, even if it's nonsense or just the words I *need an idea*, or I *don't know*, or *ugh*! It sounds silly, but this early writing is for my eyes only—it's an exercise to warm up my writing muscles.

Try freewriting the next time you're looking for writing ideas. Put your pencil on the paper and keep it moving. After a while you may find that your thoughts grab the pencil and your writing takes off.

Practice

Here's a piece from my friend Jimmy's freewriting. He starts out searching for topic ideas for a personal narrative about a favorite toy.

> **Sal's example**
>
> *The first present I ever got for Christmas that I can remember, is a small pack of hot wheels. I need an idea. I need an idea. I remember that I loved those hot wheels very much and played with them all day. I need an idea. I need an idea. But by the end of the week I was sick of them and they were all beat up. I played with a different toy then. . . .*
>
> Jimmy Crouch
> Winburn Middle School

When Jimmy freewrote, his writing took a turn and he found a new direction. He began writing about "hot wheels" and found he liked a different toy instead. To discover more about the favorite toy, he can freewrite again.

Ready-to-Go Writing Lessons That Teach Key Strategies
Scholastic Professional Books

Your Turn

Now it's your turn to warm up and see where your writing takes you. Apply your creative streak and freewrite a few lines on two of the topics below.

1. A favorite outfit or _____ (topic of your choice)

_____

_____

_____

_____

_____

_____

_____

Remember to keep the pencil moving— don't take it off the page!

2. The last time I laughed or _____ (topic of your choice)

_____

_____

_____

_____

_____

_____

_____

_____

Think of freewriting as an adventure; you can end up someplace totally different from where you started. For example, I might begin writing about an important game and end up writing about something that's even more interesting to me, like my coach's surprising decision to make our team co-ed. I bet you'll also discover new, exciting things to write about when you freewrite.

3. A person I know well or _____

(topic of your choice)

_____

_____

_____

_____

_____

_____

_____

Ready-to-Go Writing Lessons That Teach Key Strategies
Scholastic Professional Books

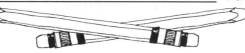

 ## Play the Game

Now that you've tried freewriting on the topics above, you probably find one topic easier to write about than the others. Pick that topic and underline or highlight words, phrases, or sentences that grab your attention. Use one or two of those underlined or highlighted parts as a topic to freewrite about again for ideas to include in a personal essay. Stay with it! (Time: five minutes)

_____

_____

_____

_____

_____

_____

_____

_____

_____

_____

_____

_____

_____

_____

_____

_____

_____

_____

_____

(Go to another sheet if you need more space.)

 ## Check It

How did it feel to freewrite? How long could you keep the pencil moving without stopping? What new words, phrases, and ideas did you discover?

_____

_____

_____

Ready-to-Go Writing Lessons That Teach Key Strategies
Scholastic Professional Books

Describing the Plays
Using Sensory Details

Flat, boring, and unoriginal. That's how writing can sound when authors neglect sensory details in their writing. One way to help students become better writers is to show them how good writers use sensory details to add interest, depth, and immediacy to their writing. This lesson alerts students to sensory details in their world and helps them use those details in their writing.

Focus Students use their five senses to gather material for writing.

Writing links Personal narrative, poetry, short story, and expository essay.

Lesson activity, pages 20–22 Students write from firsthand observations and record sensory details about a selected person, place, or object to include in a descriptive journal entry. You can choose one of the topics for the entire class to write on or allow each student to choose from the list.

Introducing the lesson Ask students to listen as you read a descriptive passage, such as the selection below from Wilson Rawls's *Where the Red Fern Grows*. You might display this narrative excerpt on the board or overhead so students can refer to specific words or phrases. Invite students to respond to the sensory details the author includes. Discuss the following: *What sensory details does the author use to help you enter this scene?* Guide students to pinpoint specific places where sensory details or descriptions make the writing come alive. Using student responses, make a class list of those sensory details.

In this passage, country boy Billy Colman discovers a playground with a long blue slide and decides to take a ride.

Laying my sack down, I started climbing up. The farther I went, the darker and more scary it got. Just as I reached the top, my feet slipped. Down I sailed. All the way down I tried to grab on to something, but there was nothing to grab. . . .

I came out just like I went in, feet first and belly down. My legs were spread out like a bean-shooter stalk. Arms flailing the air, I zoomed out and up. I seemed to hang suspended in air at the peak of my climb. I could see the hard-packed ground far below.

As I started down, I shut my eyes tight and gritted my teeth. This didn't seem to help. With a splattering sound, I landed. I felt the air whoosh out between my teeth. I tried to scream, but had no wind left to make a sound.

After bouncing a couple of times, I finally settled down to earth. I lay spread-eagled for a few seconds, and then slowly got to my knees.

Hearing loud laughter, I looked around. It was the little old lady with the hoe in her hand. She hollered and asked how I liked it. Without answering, I grabbed up my gunny sack and left. Far up the street, I looked back. The little old lady was sitting down, rocking with laughter.

Students may notice the following:

visual details darker, legs spread out like a bean-shooter stalk, hard-packed ground, little old lady with the hoe, sitting down, rocking with laughter

auditory details splattering sound, hearing loud laughter, she hollered and asked

touching details shut my eyes tight, gritted my teeth, felt the air whoosh out

Literature resource *Where the Red Fern Grows* contains many examples of sensory details. If copies of the book are available, read Chapter Five, which follows the excerpt above. In the first few pages Rawls introduces the stationmaster with the "funny little cap" who "laid his hand" on the boy's shoulder. The boy "hear[s] several puppy whimpers." Invite students to make a list of sensory details while listening to you read the chapter aloud or while reading on their own.

TIP When writers first experiment with sensory details, they may overload their writing with sounds, smells, visuals, and other details. Point out that writing with too many details is like eating an entire plate of fudge or over-salting your food—it's just too much to stomach. Refer to the passage above or to another descriptive piece to show how good authors use (but don't abuse!) sensory details.

Notes:

Ready-to-Go Writing Lessons That Teach Key Strategies
Scholastic Professional Books

Describing the Plays
Using Sensory Details

Listen Up: What are the sensory details in your writing?

Hey! Let's talk about sensory details and how you can use them like a pro in your writing. Have you ever listened to the announcer for a game? You'll recognize plenty of sensory details in this play-by-play account:

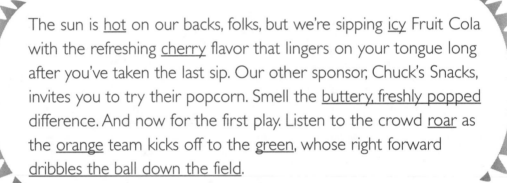

The sun is <u>hot</u> on our backs, folks, but we're sipping <u>icy</u> Fruit Cola with the refreshing <u>cherry</u> flavor that lingers on your tongue long after you've taken the last sip. Our other sponsor, Chuck's Snacks, invites you to try their popcorn. Smell the <u>buttery, freshly popped</u> difference. And now for the first play. Listen to the crowd <u>roar</u> as the <u>orange</u> team kicks off to the <u>green</u>, whose right forward <u>dribbles the ball down the field</u>.

See the sensory details I underlined? A sensory detail refers to features we can see, hear, smell, taste, and touch. Including these makes your writing more real for your reader. Now let's huddle for a quick play-by-play of the announcer's paragraph above:

Seeing   Hearing   Smelling

_____   _____   _____

_____   _____   _____

Tasting   Touching

_____   _____

_____   _____

Ready-to-Go Writing Lessons That Teach Key Strategies
Scholastic Professional Books

Practice

To make my words capture the sensory details around me, I look carefully at a person or animal, a place, or an object. As I observe details, I scribble them down in my journal. Here's one of my entries:

Sal's example

Sal's Smooth Choco-Banana Milkshake

I see	yellow skin, white clumps of banana, dark brown syrup, fudge-swirl ice cream
I hear	whir, gurgle, icky grinding of the blender
I smell	ripe banana, vanilla with medicine smell
I taste	sweet, creamy, rich mix of flavors
I touch	icy surface of the metal

Now it's time to show you my details put together in a descriptive paragraph:

My favorite treat is Sal's Famous Choco-Banana Milkshake. After peeling back the yellow skin, I chop the ripe banana into white clumps and add them to dark brown syrup, a teaspoon of vanilla—smells like medicine but it adds flavor—and fudge-swirl ice cream. I touch the icy surface of the metal cup and listen to the whir, gurgle, and icky grinding of the blender. Then I scoop up a glob and taste a sweet, rich mix of flavors.

> Sometimes your experience will not include details from all of the senses. For example, you cannot taste your backpack or your bike or your classroom or hear a room. But there are plenty of other details. Write about those.

Your Turn

Now you'll see what I mean. Circle one topic from the lists below or choose your own topic! Take your topic to the next page and record all the sensory details you observe under as many categories as you can.

Person or Animal	**Place**	**Object**
my best friend	my room	my backpack
my cat/dog/pet	my classroom	our car
a relative	the park	my bike

Ready-to-Go Writing Lessons That Teach Key Strategies
Scholastic Professional Books

My topic	I see
	• _____
	• _____
	• _____

I hear	I smell
• _____	• _____
• _____	• _____
• _____	• _____

I taste	I touch
• _____	• _____
• _____	• _____
• _____	• _____

Play the Game

Using the sensory details you collected on your topic in **Your Turn**, write a descriptive paragraph on the lines below.

_____

_____

_____

_____

_____

_____

_____

_____

_____

_____

✓ Check It

Review your descriptive paragraph and underline words that refer to sensory details: what you see, hear, smell, taste, and touch. Do they paint a clear picture of the person, place, or object you described?

Reading up on the Game

Learning from Other Writers

Read to write? Does that make sense? At least that's what students will wonder. But we teachers know that students learn excellent techniques from reading the work of favorite authors. Directed reading can help highlight these techniques: When you present questions to ask during a reading, you help students recognize good techniques so they can use them in their own writing.

Focus Students read to learn good writing techniques.

Writing links All writing.

Lesson activity, pages 25–27 The lesson introduces sample questions to guide students while reading with a purpose. Students apply questions to an excerpt found in the opening of E. L. Konigsburg's *From the Mixed-up Files of Mrs. Basil E. Frankweiler*. Then they complete a form, Learning from Other Writers, on a book, an article, or a poem.

Introducing the lesson Read aloud from an overhead the following paragraphs from "The Andy Strasberg Story" for a brief introduction to reading with a purpose. Ask the students the following questions: *What about the writing makes the paragraphs fresh and appealing? Which parts grab your interest most? Why?* As students identify the qualities they like, they also will be collecting ideas to include in their own writing.

I grew up in the shadows of Yankee Stadium—if it was a long, long shadow! We were really about five miles from the ballpark. One of my fondest memories is when my dad first took me to the Polo Grounds. In the middle of Harlem was this immense cathedral and inside was all this green, green grass. Incredible.

On that particular day the Giants were playing the Phillies and the Phillies were wearing the old-style uniforms, with the oversized red numbers on the back. My dad had purchased tickets to sit in the upper deck, general admission, and then in about the fourth inning he said, "I'll be back in just a minute," and went downstairs. I was sitting there all alone. After about fifteen minutes he came back and motioned for me to come with him and we sat down about four rows from the field. He slipped the usher some money and the guy wiped off the seat. And I just fell in love with baseball. That was 1957 when I was eight years old and throughout my life, every time I started to drift away from the game, something brought me back, something incredible, something very special.

Introduce students to questions that will help them learn from reading the words of another writer. These are questions they will encounter on pages 25–27:

✳ *How did the opening catch my attention?* Students may find the idea of growing up in the shadow of a famous place intriguing.

✳ *How did the writing hold my attention?* Students may be engaged through the clear voice ("Incredible."), the details ("old-style uniforms" and "oversized red numbers"), and the metaphor for the stadium ("cathedral"). They also may be won over by the dad's loving efforts to find a better seat.

Ready-to-Go Writing Lessons That Teach Key Strategies
Scholastic Professional Books

✳ *What did I learn from the writing?* Encourage students to respond to the writing itself. For example, call attention to the difference clear details make ("old-style uniforms" rather than "uniforms"), the value of figurative language ("cathedral" rather than "stadium"), and the benefit of reporting the series of the dad's actions leading to their good seats. Although it's important to appreciate all responses to the reading, guide students back to the writing itself.

Literature resource Students will enjoy hearing the entire opening chapter from Konigburg's *From the Mixed-up Files of Mrs. Basil E. Frankweiler* (excerpted on page 26). When you finish reading, you can ask some of the questions all over again: *How did the writer develop the chapter to hold your attention? What details, actions, and descriptions made you want to hear more? How can you adapt these to your own writing?* Also invite students to share impressions they take away from the chapter. Such questions can be applied to a variety of writing— a paragraph, an excerpt, a chapter, an article, a poem, a song, or an entire book.

TIP Reading great writing aloud in class helps students develop an ear for rhythm and style and gives the teacher another opportunity to ask questions about what makes the writing work. New and different questions will emerge with each reading. New and different answers will provide students with novel techniques to use in their own writing. Set aside a regular time in your weekly schedule for both you and your students to share favorite passages from books, magazines, newspapers, and so forth that reveal a technique or style worth trying. When students make a habit of studying the way other authors write, they undoubtedly will continue to improve their own writing.

Ready-to-Go Writing Lessons That Teach Key Strategies
Scholastic Professional Books

Name _____   Date _____

Reading up on the Game

Learning from Other Writers

Listen Up: How do you improve your writing?

Who knows most about soccer strategies and moves? Experienced players, that's who, and watching them improves my game. Who knows most about good writing? Experienced writers, that's who, and reading their work improves my writing. When I read with the eyes of a writer, I read differently from when I'm reading for pleasure. I look closely at the way an author uses words to build a story, an article, or an essay.

I ask questions to focus in on good techniques. For example, *How does this opening catch my attention*? Do I *find surprise developments, descriptive language, dialogue, or action*? *What do I learn from the writing*? *Does the writer leave me with a thought to chew on, a word picture to consider, or an action that was entertaining*? Set aside time to read with the eyes of a writer; your writing will improve.

Practice

Now let's kick into some practice and read with a purpose. When you read, ask questions about the writing:

* How did the opening catch my attention?
* How did the writing hold my attention?
* What did I learn from the writing?

Sal's example

Read the opening to this short story:

What's that buzz? That was my first thought when the alarm tripped in the drugstore. I looked around and saw customers' startled faces. All at once, we heard a shout.

How did the opening to the short story catch your attention?

_____

_____

Ready-to-Go Writing Lessons That Teach Key Strategies
Scholastic Professional Books

Your Turn

Here's an excerpt from the opening to *From the Mixed-up Files of Mrs. Basil E. Frankweiler* by E. L. Konigsburg. Practice reading with the eyes of a writer.

> Claudia knew that she could never pull off the old-fashioned kind of running away. That is, running away in the heat of anger with a knapsack on her back. She didn't like discomfort; even picnics were untidy and inconvenient: all those insects and the sun melting the icing on the cupcakes. Therefore, she decided that her leaving home would not be just running from somewhere but would be running to somewhere. To a large place, a comfortable place, an indoor place, and preferably a beautiful place. And that's why she decided upon the Metropolitan Museum of Art in New York City.

1. How did the opening catch my attention? (Check out interesting sentences and ideas in the first paragraph again.)

_____

_____

_____

_____

2. How did the writing hold my attention? (What kept me reading?)

_____

_____

_____

_____

3. What did I learn from the writing? (How does the author use words in new ways, build sentences, introduce characters, and set the stage for the action?)

_____

_____

_____

_____

Ready-to-Go Writing Lessons That Teach Key Strategies
Scholastic Professional Books

Play the Game

Choose a familiar book, article, or poem and identify some of the
writing techniques the writer uses. Your answers to the following
questions will help you and other writers see the value of reading for writing.

Learning from Other Writers

Student's Name _____ Date _____

Title _____ Author _____

How did the opening catch my attention?

_____

_____

_____

_____

What qualities of the writing held my attention?

_____

_____

_____

_____

What did I learn from the writing to use in my writing?

_____

_____

_____

_____

✔ Check It

What writing technique do you want to apply to your future writing? If you
can't think of any, go back to **Listen Up** for ideas. What other authors do you
enjoy reading? Find more of their writing to read with the eyes of a writer.

_____

_____

_____

Ready-to-Go Writing Lessons That Teach Key Strategies
Scholastic Professional Books

Your Own Playing Style

Finding the Writer's Voice

How do we teachers convince students to invest themselves in their writing? We encourage them to find and to write in their individual voices, making the page come alive with their unique ideas and experiences. The good news is that this discovery is not as difficult as many students think. It means learning to think in their own language on the page, a skill they can learn by writing aloud and then transferring the words onto the page. Then they will recognize their own writing voices.

Focus Students learn to recognize their voices on the page.

Writing links All writing.

Lesson activity, pages 29–31 To learn the sound of their voices on the page, students write out loud and on paper. First, they write a short persuasive note, then narrate a story to a classmate, and, finally, write their narrative. Later, they exchange written accounts to check for voice. (Reluctant writers or ESL students can tape-record a brief account and then transcribe it.)

Introducing the lesson We want students to be able to hear the way their speaking voices support their writing. Have each student write three sentences on one of the following topics. Urge them to make their writing sound as much as possible like their speaking.

    the last place I enjoyed visiting

    a hobby I want to take up

    a personality quirk that annoys me

When they've finished, ask the group members to fold their papers and put them in a pile. Then each group member draws one and reads it aloud. The

group tries to guess the writer. Ask the groups to consider what kinds of words, style, or ideas helped them identify the writer.

Literature resource In *The Craft of Revision*, essayist, journalist, poet, professor, and lecturer Donald Murray offers this insight on writing aloud to sense one's writer's voice.

We learned to speak before we wrote, and, even if we are writers, we speak thousands upon thousands of words more than we write in a day. When we write, we speak in written words. The magic of writing is that readers who may never meet us, hear what we have written. Music rises from the page when we read.

We call the heard quality of writing voice, and it may be the most important element in writing. Voice, like background music in a movie, is tuned to the writing, supports and extends what the writing says. . . .

TIP Students need talk time during their writing period. It's part of the process of learning the sound of their writing voices. Indeed, think of speaking as a part of writing (in fact, many famous epics, fairy tales, and fables were told out loud long before they were recorded). Allotting a few minutes of class time for students to talk out writing ideas can be a first step, a prewriting exercise, for many writing activities. In writing this book, we too talked out the lessons and the exercises as a part of the process of developing ideas and expressing them in a consistent writing voice.

Your Own Playing Style

Finding Your Writer's Voice

Listen Up: How do you write in your own voice?

When you read writing with a strong, unique voice, you hear someone behind those words, and you want to read more. As a writer, you want that same quality of realness in your writing, too. Let's look at it another way.

For me, it's the difference between losing myself in the soccer match and just showing up for the practice and the games because I *have* to. When I jump right into the game of writing, I develop my own style. Just as I have my signature moves on the field, I have my own totally individual way of writing my ideas in my own words—and the result is real writing, real for me and for my readers. I hear my own writer's voice signature on the page.

Practice

Speaking your writing aloud can help you develop your writing voice. That was my technique for the following example.

Sal's example

Mom was steamed, I could see that. How dare I wear jeans with ripped knees to school! There was a standoff in the kitchen. My heart was pumping and then my ride honked. I rocketed out the door.

Do you hear me, rather than just plain words on the page? Compare my example above with this version:

My mother and I argued about the jeans I wore because they were ripped at the knees.

Sure, this is correct writing, but it gives no sense of a real speaker. These words could be anybody's.

Ready-to-Go Writing Lessons That Teach Key Strategies
Scholastic Professional Books

Your Turn

You want to host a video party on Friday night, but you need to persuade your family through a short note. Throw your voice on the page. Speak the words aloud first and then write them on the page.

_____

_____

_____

_____

_____

_____

_____

_____

_____

_____

_____

Play the Game

It's time to try out your writing moves and learn more about the sound of your writer's voice. Choose a recent experience to "write out loud." Take three minutes to tell your story to a classmate who will listen carefully. When you finish, have your partner tell your story back to you as close as possible to the way you told it. Can you hear your voice? Now transcribe your story onto the page.

My Personal Narrative

_____

_____

_____

_____

_____

_____

_____

_____

Ready-to-Go Writing Lessons That Teach Key Strategies
Scholastic Professional Books

_____

_____

_____

_____

_____

_____

_____

_____

_____

_____

> Another useful
> way to capture
> your voice is to
> record your
> narrative on tape.
> Then play it back
> and transcribe
> your words onto
> paper.

_____

_____

_____

_____

_____

_____

_____

_____

✓ Check It

Underline places where your writing voice shines through. Ask your partner to help you find words, phrases, and passages that do and do not sound like you. Make changes to fit your voice.

Ready-to-Go Writing Lessons That Teach Key Strategies
Scholastic Professional Books

Team Talk

Capturing Dialogue

Who said that? Don't we teachers often wonder? And we can usually tell because we recognize many of our students—as well as friends, coworkers, and family members—by their particular speech patterns. Students already recognize different speakers, too, but need to learn to identify those differences and use them to enliven their writing.

Focus Students learn to recognize and record differences among speakers to work dialogue material into their writing.

Writing links Personal narrative, short story, essay, and drama.

Lesson activity, pages 34–37 Students first list words and expressions they use and like and connect them with the dialogue components of vocabulary, vernacular, and variety (student definitions, page 35). Then, in a dialogue journal (page 36), they collect a rich sampling of speech. Later, students identify the three V's in their journals. Finally, they write a one-page script with the option of incorporating some of the best samples from the journal activity.

Note: To follow up this lesson, help students integrate the rich dialogue they've captured into other writing, such as personal narratives, essays, and short stories.

Introducing the lesson A bit of drama will help students hear speech differences. Have several students act out the scene of a student cutting into the lunch line. What kinds of speech are evident as they wrangle over their disagreements and ideas? Then choose two classmates to play the adult cafeteria monitor and the assistant principal who intervene and help settle the dispute. After the encounter is over, discuss with the class the differences in speech among the characters. You may find it helps to list on the board some of the differences students notice; students can begin a dialogue journal and record them there.

Literature resource Display an excerpt from a play to show students correct script formats. Also read lines from a couple of plays to show how speech differences help define characters. Here's an example from Neil Simon's *Lost in Yonkers*. Arty is a teenager living with relatives in New York during World War II. His Uncle Louie is running from the mob and has slipped in to stay awhile. He's convincing Arty to eat the medicinal soup Grandma has prepared.

Louie: *Ever hear of General Rommel?*

Arty: *Who?*

Louie: *General Irwin Rommel. German tank commander. Right now he's rollin' right across Egypt, cuttin' through the whole British army. Tough as they come . . . But if Momma wanted him to eat the soup, he would eat the soup.*

Arty: *Did you eat it when you were a kid?*

Louie: *Oh, yeah.*

Arty: *I thought you weren't afraid of her.*

Louie: *I wasn't. That's how I proved it to her. I hated that soup worse than you. But I would drink three bowls of it and ask for more. She knew she couldn't win with me.*

Ready-to-Go Writing Lessons That Teach Key Strategies
Scholastic Professional Books

Arty: *I wish I was as tough as you.*

Louie: *Hey, you're gettin' there. You took her on, kid.*
             That took guts. That took moxie.

Arty: *What's moxie?*

Another script students may enjoy is adapted from
Barbara Robinson's novel *The Best Christmas Pageant
Ever* in *Plays Children Love, Vol. II, A Treasury of
Contemporary & Classic Plays for Children.* Call atten-
tion to differences in speech among the adults, the
main character Beth, and the terrible Herdmans.

TIP This exercise is a mere beginning
for a lifelong habit of listening for differences
among speakers. Have students return to the
dialogue journal regularly to record and discuss
the dialogue they hear in everyday life (in the car,
at the dinner table, in the school hallway, in the
lunch line, and so forth). This will heighten their
listening and writing skills.

Notes:

Team Talk
Capturing Dialogue

Listen Up: Who said that?

At half time, we players huddle around the coach. During our team talk I hear a lot of different speakers. Even if I close my eyes, I recognize their speech: Juan, who congratulates a teammate's tie-breaking kick with "Exceptional!"; Shanelle, who says "Gotcha" as the coach instructs; and Kim, who interrupts with "Oh, I understand, you mean we should. . . ."

The words and expressions each person chooses create a unique voice signature. When you capture the individual voices among speakers, your writing comes alive. You'll attempt to copy or imitate each speaker as carefully as possible so that his or her words are authentic and the writing feels real.

List some expressions and words you like to use:

Practice

When I'm listening for differences among speakers, I remember the three V's.

Ready-to-Go Writing Lessons That Teach Key Strategies
Scholastic Professional Books

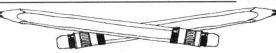

Sal's example

The 3 V's—A Key to Real Dialogue

Vo-cab-u-lary: Do you sometimes hear words (or read them in a book) that make you sit up and take notice? Maybe you think of them as "dictionary words" because you have to look them up to understand what they mean. For example, instead of *sat*, have you heard someone say *perched* or *hunkered*? Maybe you've heard a friend talk computer language—*download*, *crash*, and *byte*. Open your ears to strong vocabulary; you might learn the perfect word to use in your future writing.

Vernacular: What everyday expressions do you use? Is your cap *cool*? If your mother's like mine, she says *good-looking*. Your grandfather might declare it *spiffy*. Another speaker would call it *bueno*. Or maybe your friend says *totally awesome*. Listen for the speaking style of the groups you hang around as well as other groups and spice up your dialogue by using these different styles.

Variety: Do you listen for differences in the kinds of sentences people put together? Some sentences are short and choppy; others are long and rambling. Some are simple and others are complex. For example, a toddler may insist, "I want cookie." A more mature speaker knows how to ask for something differently, depending on the situation. You may hear a player beg the coach at practice, "If I run an extra three laps, can I please leave ten minutes early?" Or you may hear a confident, "Gotta split, Coach." Listen for sentence variety among speakers and try to use it in your own writing.

Your Turn

Begin a dialogue journal. First, listen, listen, listen to the conversations around you. Then, try to record the actual words, phrases, and sentences of the speakers you hear during the school day. Start by collecting speech samples you have heard in class. Carry your journal with you and collect samples throughout the day—snippets from conversations among adults and peers at school, from TV and radio shows, and from around home. As your journal grows, you might want to compare it with a friend's, looking for the three V's in the speech samples. Here's a page to get you started on your dialogue journal.

> Remember, write exactly what you hear. Principals, teachers, librarians, lunchroom workers, and your friends have different ways of speaking and are valuable sources of excellent dialogue.

Ready-to-Go Writing Lessons That Teach Key Strategies
Scholastic Professional Books

Dialogue Journal

Write the speakers' names below.   Write the words of each speaker on the lines at the right.

_____ :   _____

Speaker 1   _____

_____

_____

_____

_____

_____

_____

_____

_____

_____

_____

_____

_____

_____

_____

_____

_____

_____

_____

_____

_____

_____

Listen for the three V's: **vocabulary** (Are special types of words being used?), **vernacular** (What style is the speaker using?), and **variety** (Are the sentences long or short? Simple or complex?)

Ready-to-Go Writing Lessons That Teach Key Strategies
Scholastic Professional Books

Play the Game

You probably know that drama is dialogue telling a story. Actors in plays, on TV, and in movies use scripts, a writing form that lists speakers and their lines. The best lines show differences in speech—and you've learned to listen for these. Reflect your new skills in a one-page script of a lunch line drama. Try to incorporate some of the speech samples from your journal.

Lunch Line Rumble

_____: _____
Speaker 1

    _____

    _____

    _____

    _____

    _____

    _____

    _____

    _____

    _____

    _____

    _____

    _____

    _____

    _____

    _____

    _____

    _____

    _____

    _____

    _____

Check It

Read your script aloud. Identify and underline your examples of the three V's.

Ready-to-Go Writing Lessons That Teach Key Strategies
Scholastic Professional Books

The Game from Inside

Revealing the Writer's Thoughts and Feelings

"Just the facts, ma'am. Just the facts." Is that all readers want—a report of events, a list of actions, or a description of people and places? Of course not. They want writing that also reveals what's going through the writer's heart and mind. So how can we help young writers weave their ideas and emotions about a topic into their writing? We urge them to reveal what they think and feel about their topic. This emotional and intellectual depth adds a rich layer of meaning to our students' work. And the result is powerful writing.

Focus Students learn to reveal their thinking and feeling in their writing.

Writing links Personal narrative, poetry, essay, and drama.

Lesson activity, pages 39–41 Students select a memory, connect it to specific feelings, and list words and phrases associated with the memory. Using these words and phrases, they craft a short free-verse poem.

Introducing the lesson Do what teacher and author Katie Ray recommends and string together an instant poem. Focus this writing activity around a particular emotion such as frustration, anger, loneliness, or excitement. Have students select a favorite phrase from a poem, a book, or their own writing that matches the target emotion. Then the class, as a whole or in small groups, reads the lines through, creating a single piece out of many parts. It's amazing to hear the kinds of discussions that evolve out of this work—about what lines fit particularly well together, what seem to be ending or beginning lines, what rhythms emerge. Urge students to rearrange the lines to improve their instant poem; eventually someone can record it.

Manipulating the words and combinations of words empowers students to handle language and sharpens their ability to express the targeted emotions.

Literature resource In the first stanza of Ted Hughes's poem "The Thought-Fox," the speaker expresses his thoughts through the words "I imagine" and projects his own feeling of loneliness onto the clock ("clock's loneliness"):

> *I imagine this midnight moment's forest:*
> *Something else is alive*
> *Beside the clock's loneliness*
> *And this blank page where my fingers move.*

Writing student Allison Crutcher has learned that investing her writing with her feelings empowers it:

One of my literary pieces, "Fields of Daffodils," . . . is filled with emotion. I've learned that when I care about something and show it in my writing, the reader begins to care about it as well; this has made me a much better writer.

Allison Crutcher
Winburn Middle School

TIP We must remember that although feelings and ideas are universal, the words we use to describe them are not. For students who need help naming emotions, devise a game of charades. Working as teams, students must guess or match the label for each emotion another group has acted out (for instance, students might act out crying to show sadness). In addition to strengthening ways to identify and express thoughts and feelings, this exercise builds vocabulary.

The Game from Inside

Revealing Your Thoughts and Feelings

Listen Up: How do you reveal your thoughts and feelings in your writing?

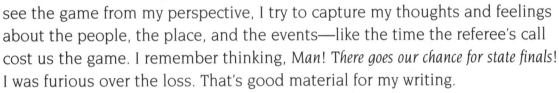

At game time I'm too excited and involved to think about what's going on. But later, when I want to write about that game and help my readers see the game from my perspective, I try to capture my thoughts and feelings about the people, the place, and the events—like the time the referee's call cost us the game. I remember thinking, Man! *There goes our chance for state finals!* I was furious over the loss. That's good material for my writing.

When I need help naming and describing my thoughts and feelings, I brainstorm to make a connection in my writing between the game outside—the players, the field, and the action—and the game inside—my opinions, reactions, thoughts, and feelings about what happened on the field. You can do the same when you write about important issues and events in your life.

Practice

It helps to choose a memory that really makes you want to write, a time that stirred up your thoughts and feelings. Here's my example to show you how it works.

> **Sal's example**
>
> Memory: first day back to school
>
> Thoughts: miss the pool already; wish my best friend and I were in the same Spanish class; don't want to have to do homework tonight
>
> Feelings: scared, confused, excited, happy, cautious, shy

Ready-to-Go Writing Lessons That Teach Key Strategies
Scholastic Professional Books

Your Turn

My memory _____

What do you remember thinking and feeling? Jot down a quick list of the thoughts and feelings you identify with that time (follow my example on page 39).

Thoughts: _____

_____

_____

Feelings: _____

_____

_____

If you get stuck, think about your first day of school, a move to a new home or school, a time you were lost, an injury, or a birthday party.

Now take five to ten minutes to expand your memory by listing words and phrases that will make your memory come alive and take your reader into the scene. Close your eyes and picture exactly where you were, who was there, and what happened (don't forget those sensory details that will ignite your reader's senses). You might include a description of the scene and people involved, as well as their actions and conversations. Use these details to express the thoughts and feelings that you listed above.

_____

_____

_____

_____

_____

_____

_____

_____

_____

_____

_____

_____

_____

Ready-to-Go Writing Lessons That Teach Key Strategies
Scholastic Professional Books

Play the Game

Poetry helps writers to connect their thoughts and feelings with their experiences. Here's your chance to make your own connection through writing a poem. First, reread your description from **Your Turn**. Highlight words and phrases that express the thoughts and feelings closest to the way you experienced them in the memory. Second, copy five to ten of your favorite highlighted words and phrases onto a separate sheet of paper and cut them out. Spread each word or phrase out on a blank page, and play with their order until you craft a free-verse poem (don't worry about rhyme or meter). Fourth, read through your poem and add a word here and there to help the poem flow and make sense. Finally, copy your poem below.

_____
_____
_____
_____
_____
_____
_____
_____
_____
_____
_____
_____
_____
_____
_____
_____

> Take a look at this poem by Langston Hughes. What feelings are embedded in the lines?
>
> **Subway Rush Hour**
> Mingled
> breath and smell
> so close
> mingled
> black and white
> so near
> no room for fear.

mingled

so near

black and white

no room for fear

Check It

Move the order of your words and phrases to create another poem.
Does the new arrangement create new feelings?

Ready-to-Go Writing Lessons That Teach Key Strategies
Scholastic Professional Books

Spectators and Fans

Writing for an Audience

"What's the big deal about audience? I don't care what everybody thinks! I just write what I think." Students who make statements like these are right, to some extent. But we teachers know that good writing needs to be shared and is usually targeted for a specific audience. This is one of those principles that students act on in everyday life without necessarily realizing it. They switch easily from friend to teacher to parent when they speak, changing content, descriptions, expressions, and words. They will want to—and in many cases, need to—do the same in their writing.

Focus Students learn that audience influences their choices of content, descriptions, expressions, and words in their writing.

Writing links Personal narrative, poetry, short story, persuasive essay, letter, and drama.

Lesson activity, pages 44–46 Students write letters to specific audiences: a teacher, a grandparent, and a friend. A follow-up discussion allows them to compare differences between the two letters in terms of content, words, descriptions, and expressions.

Introducing the lesson The following excerpts, both written by Lucy Maud Montgomery, show the distinct difference keeping an audience in mind makes in one's writing. Present both passages and ask students to identify content, descriptions, expressions, and word choice as they point to a particular audience.

Dear Mr. MacMillan:
. . . My life has had its share—sometimes I am tempted as now to feel more than its share of worries and trials and sorrows. But I haven't really said much about them in my letters, have I? Well, I'm afraid I'm going to break my record. I am afraid that this letter, no matter how much I shall assuredly try to make it what I would like it to be, will not be a very cheerful or inspirational epistle. (My Dear Mr. M: Letters to G. B. MacMillan from L. M. Montgomery)

Compare the above with this passage from Montgomery's *Anne of Avonlea* where the writer's choices create a voice for her different audience:

Oh, this is a day left over from Eden, isn't it, Diana? . . . The Air has magic in it. Look at the purple in the cup of that harvest valley, Diana. And oh, do smell the dying fir! It's coming up from that little sunny hollow where Mr. Eben Wright has been cutting fence poles.

Ask who the different audiences are for the two passages and what words in the writing give clues about who is being addressed. Students will recognize that the first letter is written for an adult friend and the second passage is written for the author's Anne Shirley fans, who would expect a lighthearted, romantic story in an idyllic setting.

Literature resource Collect magazines from the school or public library to help students

Ready-to-Go Writing Lessons That Teach Key Strategies
Scholastic Professional Books

recognize differences in writing for a variety of audiences. Move beyond the obvious pictures and ads to study the language. Find examples of how age, gender, and interest influence the writing. Look closely at content, descriptions, expressions, word choice, and, when appropriate, length. Collect an assortment of magazines that show a wide variety of audience appeal, such as *Cricket, Scope, ESPN, PC World, Majesty, Yankee, Guitar, Sports Illustrated for Kids, American Craft, Southern Living, Family Fun, Ranger Rick, Highlights, National Geographic,* and *AARP* magazine.

TIP The concept of audience extends beyond writing. We find the idea in TV programs and movies as well. Rating systems identify intended audiences by established criteria, and students are keenly aware of this. Ask them how they could tell a G from a PG or PG-13 movie without knowing the rating. Relate this back to the idea of writing for an audience: What might be appropriate language, content, and style in a note to a friend might not be acceptable for a letter of excuse to a teacher or principal.

Notes:

Spectators and Fans

Writing for an Audience

Listen Up: Who is your audience?

Hey Writer Pal,

Remember this. It's important. When you write, you have to think about who your audience is. You need to keep your readers in mind when you decide what ideas or content to add.

Ask yourself: *What words, descriptions, or expressions will make sense to this particular reader? How will I express myself if I want to be taken seriously?* and *How much should I write?* For example, think about the differences between notes you might send to your friend and to your teacher. In each case you have a different reading audience—each with different ideas and expectations.

Your writing pal,
Soccer Sal

Practice

Here's an example of knowing your audience.

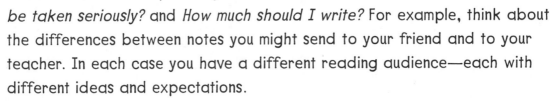

Sal's example
Nathaniel—

I'm in deep, deep trouble. The homework bandit struck again and I don't have my notes for the test. Save my neck!!! I'm begging for your notes, buddy. Call me.
                                                                    —Sal

Who is my audience?

_____

What clues from my note told you this?

_____

44

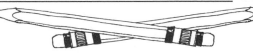

Your Turn

Trouble! The teacher intercepted my note to Nathaniel. Step into my cleats and write a letter to my teacher Ms. Jane Bond explaining what happened to the notes and asking permission to make up the assignment. Remember, this different audience will affect your choice of words, descriptions, and expressions. Good luck—she's tough.

Dear Ms. Bond,

_____

_____

_____

_____

_____

_____

_____

_____

_____

_____

_____

_____

_____

_____

_____

_____

_____

_____

_____

Here are three key questions to ask yourself when you write:

1. What words, descriptions, or expressions will make sense to this particular reader?

2. How will I express myself if I want to be taken seriously?

3. How much should I write?

Sincerely,
Your student Sal

Ready-to-Go Writing Lessons That Teach Key Strategies
Scholastic Professional Books

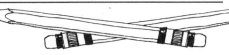

Play the Game

Choose a topic for a letter-story to two different audiences, first to a parent or an older relative and then to a friend. Notice the differences in the words, descriptions, and expressions that you choose to use in the two letters.

My letter topic _____

Dear _____ (parent/relative),

_____

_____

_____

_____

_____

_____

_____

_____

_____

_____

_____

Dear _____ (friend),

_____

_____

_____

_____

_____

_____

_____

_____

_____

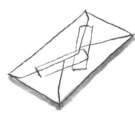

Be on the lookout for writing topics that pop up in your writing and in the world around you: a surprise from your friend, a recent success, a pet, your best game, an accident, a friend you helped, your family, or anything else from your life.

✓ Check It

What makes these two letters different? Underline words, details, and expressions that show how each letter appeals to your different audiences.

Ready-to-Go Writing Lessons That Teach Key Strategies
Scholastic Professional Books

Making a Game Plan
Organizing the Writing

We've all seen the typical middle school writing—an extended opening, an underdeveloped middle, and a truncated ending. But we know there's a better way. We know that any writing must begin quickly, develop well, and finish with a flourish to satisfy the reader. This lesson offers a structure to help students organize their writing effectively.

Focus Students learn to organize their writing into an opening, a middle, and an ending.

Writing links Personal narrative, short story, essay, and drama.

Lesson activity, pages 49–51 Using the pencil graphic organizer on page 48, students organize and freewrite their ideas for an autobiographical essay on a trip.

Note: The writing students produce in this lesson can be used to support Lesson 11: *Pulling Your Game Together, Composing a Rough Draft.*

Introducing the lesson Ask students to choose and briefly discuss a favorite book in terms of its structure—opening, middle, and ending. Then draw a visual organizer in the shape of a pencil on the board or on an overhead transparency.

Note the parts and their descriptions:

Point—the **opening**: keen, sharp, and to the point

Length—the **middle**: longest part, extended and developed

Eraser— the **ending**: short, final, and satisfying

Literature resource Readers look for order in any writing, so the events or progression of the writing must be clear. Short stories and essays can illustrate great openings, middles, and endings. (See page 48.)

Opening: The opening may be a single sentence, a group of sentences, or even a single word that reaches out and grabs the reader's attention. The opening extends far enough to set up the whole piece, whether it introduces a story's characters or conflict, an essay's central idea, or a personal narrative's opening events.

Middle: The middle part of the writing, the largest section, builds on the foundation set by the opening. Most of the writing happens here: The story's characters and conflict develop, the essay's central idea expands, and the personal narrative's events unfold.

Ending: At last the writer hints at the ending ahead. The rule of thumb is to end quickly because once the reader sees the ending ahead, there's little else to say. A good ending satisfies the reader and the writer. You know a powerful ending when you read one! It's a *wow!* or a *yes!*—just like the finish of a strong game.

> **TIP** Both the writer and the reader can lose their way in the middle of a piece. For example, in a reflective letter, Sarah Schaefer commented on the difficulties of "middles."
>
> *I've been told that the middle is the most important part of the story. It's where the most exciting events occur. Unfortunately, I have somewhat of a hard time developing it into a suspenseful segment. The middles of my stories usually slump as sometimes I get off the topic into irrelevant topics that the reader doesn't really care for. In this area, the problem is very hard to correct.*
> Sarah L. Schaefer
> Winburn Middle School

Ready-to-Go Writing Lessons That Teach Key Strategies
Scholastic Professional Books

Making a Game Plan

Organizing Your Writing

Here, the pencil organizer shows the structure of a narrative.

Point—the *opening*, keen and sharp

For Sparky, school was all but impossible. He failed every subject in the eighth grade. He flunked physics in high school, getting a grade of zero. Sparky also flunked Latin, algebra and English. He didn't do much better in sports. Although he did manage to make the school's golf team, he promptly lost the only important match of the season. There was a consolation match; he lost that, too.

Length—the *middle*, longest part, extended and developed

Sparky was a loser. He, his classmates . . . everyone knew it. So he rolled with it. Sparky had made up his mind early in life that if things were meant to work out, they would. Otherwise he would content himself with what appeared to be his inevitable mediocrity.

However, one thing was important to Sparky—drawing. He was proud of his artwork. Of course, no one else appreciated it. In his senior year of high school, he submitted some cartoons to the editors of the yearbook. The cartoons were turned down. Despite this particular rejection, Sparky was so convinced of his ability that he decided to become a professional artist.

After completing high school, he wrote a letter to Walt Disney Studios. He was told to send some samples of his artwork, and the subject for a cartoon was suggested. Sparky drew the proposed cartoon. He spent a great deal of time on it and on all the other drawings he submitted. Finally, the reply came from Disney Studios. He had been rejected once again. Another loss for the loser.

Eraser—the *ending*, short and final

So Sparky decided to write his own autobiography in cartoons. He described his childhood self—a little boy loser and chronic underachiever. The cartoon character would soon become famous worldwide. For Sparky . . . was Charles Schulz. He created the "Peanuts" comic strip and the little cartoon character whose kite would never fly and who never succeeded in kicking a football, Charlie Brown.

(from "Sparky" by Earl Nightengale, cited in *Chicken Soup for the Teenage Soul*)

Ready-to-Go Writing Lessons That Teach Key Strategies
Scholastic Professional Books

Making a Game Plan

Organizing Your Writing

Listen Up: How can you organize your writing?

Organization helps when you write, just like it helps when my team plans each game. Whether it's soccer on the field—my favorite—or checkers on the board, there's a clear order of moves the players choose for the best game. A game begins with a swift start, develops in the middle into a number of strategies and moves, and then ends quickly with victory for somebody.

Organizing your writing keeps it clear for both you and your reader, from your opening through to your ending. Good organization is your key to scoring a writing victory.

Practice

How do you organize? Well, I'm writing a personal narrative on "My Trip to the Ballpark" and all I know is I have a lot of material to write about and to tie together into one story. Then I take a good look at my pencil and come up with the answer.

Sal's example

opening
Wow! Stadium is huge but finally find seats

middle
1. our team behind—star player is out
2. sudden unexpected goal by rookie—game tied
3. crowd cheering   hugging   what a feeling
4. lady beside me gives me high five

ending
My cousin and I run down to get autographs

Ready-to-Go Writing Lessons That Teach Key Strategies
Scholastic Professional Books

Your Turn

Using the pencil graphic, organize the events of a trip you took—to the corner store, to the theme park, to the mountains, or to any place. Think about how the trip began, choose three to four important events to develop, and tie it all together with a great ending.

opening _____

_____

_____

_____

middle _____

_____

_____

_____

_____

_____

_____

_____

Don't worry about writing in complete sentences when you're organizing. Just list your ideas in a way you'll be able to use them later when you write the rough draft.

ending _____

_____

_____

_____

_____

_____

Ready-to-Go Writing Lessons That Teach Key Strategies
Scholastic Professional Books

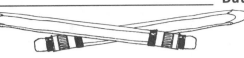

Play the Game

Using your pencil organizer, freewrite about your trip. That means writing all you can, following your notes from the organizer, without lifting your pencil from the page. You might use this freewriting to write the rough draft.

_____

_____

_____

_____

_____

_____

_____

_____

_____

_____

_____

_____

_____

_____

_____

_____

_____

_____

_____

_____

 Check It

On your freewriting, box out what may become the opening, middle, and ending of your future rough draft. Label these parts O, M, and E.

Ready-to-Go Writing Lessons That Teach Key Strategies
Scholastic Professional Books

The Right Kickoff

Writing Compelling Openings

Just a few seconds to catch the reader's interest! That's what some experts say the writer has. In a great opening, the first lines reach out and "hook" the reader. Students must learn that in this technologically rapid world readers do not hang around long—you could say that the opening is like an advertisement for the piece. Students must learn to capture their reader's attention as quickly as possible; they must move beyond the familiar "It was a dark and stormy night" to an opening that shouts, "Read this!"

Focus Students learn to craft openings that hook their readers.

Writing links Personal narrative, short story, essay, and drama.

Lesson activity, pages 53–55 Students brainstorm ideas for a persuasive letter and then craft several different openings that will catch the reader's attention. They select their best opening and organize their thoughts to compose a draft of the letter.

Introducing the lesson It's the unexpected that catches the reader's attention. To spark a reader's interest, the writer can introduce a question, a description, an unusual statement or quotation, or an action. Demonstrate the variety of ways authors can appeal to their readers by reading aloud the following openings to your students. Ask them to identify the different techniques each author used to grab the reader's attention. Then discuss briefly what makes these openings work or not work.

Dramatic Description
In a hole in the ground there lived a hobbit. Not a nasty, dirty, wet hole, filled with the ends of worms and an oozy smell, nor yet a dry, bare, sandy hole with nothing in it to sit down on or to eat: it was a hobbit-hole, and that means comfort. (From *The Hobbit: Or There and Back Again* by J. R. R. Tolkien)

Surprising Statement
What they don't understand about birthdays and what they never tell you is that when you're eleven, you're also ten, and nine, and eight, and seven, and six, and five, and four, and three, and two, and one. And when you wake up on your eleventh birthday, you expect to feel eleven, but you don't. ("Eleven" by Sandra Cisneros)

Amazing Action
They murdered him.
As he turned to take the ball, a dam burst against the side of his head and a hand grenade shattered his stomach. Engulfed by nausea, he pitched toward the grass. His mouth encountered gravel, and he spat frantically, afraid that some of his teeth had been knocked out. Rising to his feet, he saw the field through drifting gauze but held on until everything settled into place, like a lens focusing, making the world sharp again, with edges. (*The Chocolate War* by Robert Cormier)

Catchy Question
Well, if you want to know the truth, and I guess you do, I mean, what would be the point in lying about it now? ("Miracle at Clement's Pond" by Patricia Pendergraft)

Literature resource Bill Bryson's *A Walk in the Woods*, a nonfiction work, features a long opening sentence that hooks the reader followed by another paragraph with sentence variety, incisive vocabulary, and a distinctive voice. Invite students to examine Bryson's opening or that of any book, story, poem, or article and decide which category it falls into. Encourage them to use these published pieces as models for their own creative openings.

> **TIP** It's not always easy to produce a clever opening on demand. Sometimes it helps to return and revise the opening after the writing of the rough draft is underway.

Ready-to-Go Writing Lessons That Teach Key Strategies
Scholastic Professional Books

The Right Kickoff
Writing Compelling Openings

Listen Up: How do I open?

"Open?" you ask. "Do you mean in a game or in writing?" The answer is both. You open with a powerful kick to your readers that surprises them and pulls them in. A question, a description, an idea, or an action will do the job. Tossing in the unexpected word, phrase, or sentence hooks your readers' curiosity and makes them want to keep reading.

Practice

So, how do you kick off your own writing in a new way? Here are some openings that I've written to introduce a paragraph on recycling.

Sal's examples

CATCHY QUESTION
How would you like to build a mansion from trash items? Believe it or not, I've seen photographs of one.

Dramatic Description
A crystal trail of shattered glass, newsprint wind-glued against the green metal siding, and heaps of cans bulging from soggy paper bags. Disgusting, I thought as I walked up to the trash bin in the back of our apartment. And to think it was all a waste.

Surprising Statement
The concept of recycling is not a new one. Our grandparents and great-grandparents crafted clothes from old remnants of material and cultivated compost heaps from food scraps, all in an effort to reuse their materials.

AMAZING ACTION
Maddie finished her soda, reared back, and tossed the can in an arc, right into the trash can. Clunk. Made it for two points. But she missed a golden opportunity to recycle.

Ready-to-Go Writing Lessons That Teach Key Strategies
Scholastic Professional Books

Your Turn

The editors of your school or local newspaper are calling for persuasive letters about a school dress code for the opinion/editorial page. Let's brainstorm ideas about this controversial topic (or find another topic that you have a strong opinion about). Find a partner or a small group of classmates, huddle, and map out ideas for your letter supporting or opposing a school dress code (or your topic).

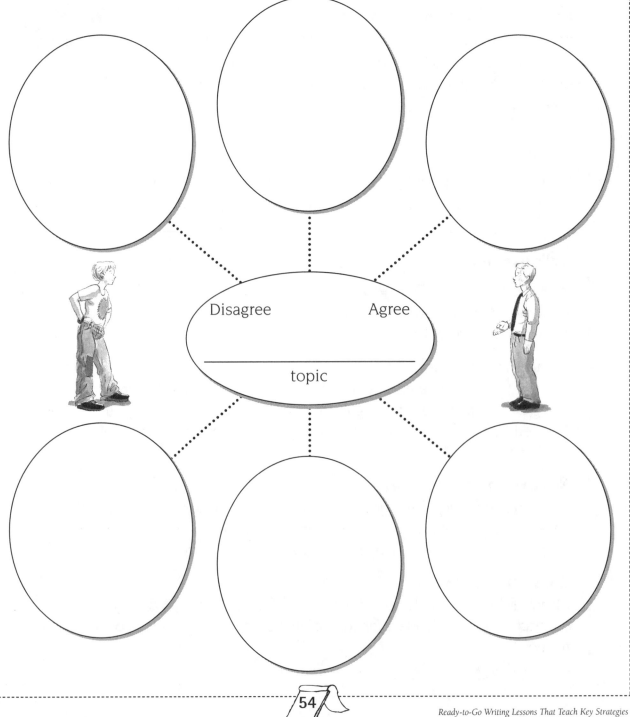

Disagree   Agree

_____

topic

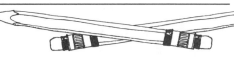

Play the Game

It's time to experiment with at least three possible openings for your persuasive letter. In the spaces below, try three—or all four!—different ways to open your letter and capture your reader's attention. Be creative and convincing!

CATCHY QUESTION _____

_____

_____

_____

Dramatic Description _____

_____

_____

_____

> A persuasive letter informs and attempts to convince the reader about an issue that you, the writer, have strong feelings about. You want to influence the reader's thoughts and actions.

Surprising Statement _____

_____

_____

_____

AMAZING ACTION _____

_____

_____

_____

Check It

Select your strongest, catchiest opening from above and write three important points that support your opinion. Use your organizer on page 54 to help you.

1. _____

2. _____

3. _____

When you're finished, write a draft of the letter that includes your best opening and the points above. Send a final draft of the letter to the editor of your school or local newspaper and see what kind of response you get!

Ready-to-Go Writing Lessons That Teach Key Strategies
Scholastic Professional Books

Pulling Your Game Together

Writing a Rough Draft

After helping students observe their world, take notes, establish a clear idea, organize, develop compelling openings, and freewrite, we send them back to their seats and tell them to get it all together in a rough draft. It's like a coach who sends the players on the soccer field, shouting, "Remember everything I've told you!" Creating the rough draft from all of these pieces can be confusing to the student, now alone with the blank page. Here's how to help.

Focus Students learn to write a rough draft from their freewriting.

Writing links Personal narrative, poetry, short story, essay, and drama.

Lesson activity, pages 58–60 Students reread their freewriting for a main idea, check for organization, expand their freewriting, craft a catchy opening, and write the rough draft.

Note: This lesson requires students to use previous freewriting and organizational work from Lesson 9: *Making a Game Plan, Organizing Your Writing.*

Introducing the lesson Warming up to the rough draft means reviewing. You can assist students individually by reviewing with them their freewriting and notes (Lesson 2), their organizer (Lesson 9), and their trial openings (Lesson 10) before they embark on a rough draft. Ideas will flow from this overview of all the writing they have at hand. Here's a mnemonic device to help students remember the steps a writer should take to write a rough draft:

Rough Draft Essentials

Assemble and review your freewriting notes.

Establish a main idea for your draft and outline the structure on an organizer.

Insert words, phrases, and sentences to expand the freewriting and delete unnecessary parts.

Open with a "hook" to catch your reader.

Use your expanded freewriting, opening, and organizer to construct a rough draft.

Literature resource Students will benefit from seeing freewriting take shape and develop into a rough draft.

An excerpt from a student sample:
Here we've taken an example of freewriting through the stages of developing a rough draft.

Ⓐ Assemble and review your freewriting notes.

As we started to go to the enormos ship I started to get very happy. We (our family) got out our lugauge and went to get our tickets. When we boarded the ship I look down the long hall ways full of people opening their room doors and entering. When we got in our room all the towels were folded into animals and we got candy under our pillows. I wanted to see what was around so I got in the elevator (I was surprised there was an elevator on a ship) to go the lobby.

Anthony Schmidt
Winburn Middle School

Ⓔ Establish a main idea for your draft and outline the structure on an organizer.
After rereading his writing, Anthony could find

Ready-to-Go Writing Lessons That Teach Key Strategies
Scholastic Professional Books

the focus, "Cruising for Surprises," and then reorganize his ideas on the pencil organizer. The third sentence could become his first event.

I **Insert words, phrases, and sentences to expand the freewriting and delete unnecessary parts.**
Notice the additions and deletions Anthony could make to focus on his main idea.

~~As we started to go to the enormous ship I started to get very happy. We (our family) got out our lugauge and went to get our tickets.~~ When we boarded the ship I look down the long hall ways <u>and was surprised to see</u> ~~full of~~ people <u>everywhere</u> opening their room doors and entering, <u>laughing, calling out to each other, and carrying even more lugauge than we were. I never expected to find swans and bears waiting for me on my bed,</u> but when we got in our room all the towels were folded into animals and, <u>even better,</u> we got candy under our pillows. <u>This was just a preview.</u> I wanted to see what else was around so I got in the elevator (I was surprised there was an elevator on a ship) to go the lobby.

O **Open with a "hook" to catch your reader.**
Adding a catchy opening increases the appeal of Anthony's writing.

When my parents announced, "We're going on a cruise!" I moaned, "Oh, no. Borrring." But was I wrong. It was seven days full of surprises, beginning with the first minute on board.

U **Use your expanded freewriting, opening, and organizer to construct a rough draft.**
Remember, in the rough draft, just as in freewriting, the writer ignores—with the teacher's permission—the common rules of grammar, punctuation, and spelling and works on building a good narrative on paper.

> **TIP** A rough draft is practice, not a final product. At this stage, we use the word *rough* over and over to encourage the creative process. You may want to invite students to freewrite their entire draft, a technique called "flashdrafting." Flashdrafting enables the student to string together lots of ideas quickly on paper and especially helps overwhelmed and reluctant writers. They can go back to their organizer and other notes after this quick writing and start revising.

Ready-to-Go Writing Lessons That Teach Key Strategies
Scholastic Professional Books

Pulling Your Game Together
Writing a Rough Draft

Listen Up: How do you develop a rough draft?

When I dash onto the field for a game, I remember practice moves, my coach's advice, our game plan, and the strategies I've learned. I bring these into the rough-and-tumble of my game—from the first kick to the final blow of the whistle.

In the same way, I have to use all of my writing skills and knowledge when I sit down to write a rough draft. But rough is the key word. Remember that a rough draft is not a polished or finished product. To develop a rough draft, first reread your freewriting and decide on a main idea. Then, check your organizer, expand your freewriting, and craft a catchy opening. Finally, shape your thoughts on the page.

Practice

Before I write a rough draft, I review my freewriting, looking for places to insert words, phrases, or sentences to expand the freewriting. Let's take an excerpt from my freewriting on "My Trip to the Ballpark."

> Forget about perfect spelling, punctuation, and grammar for now. There's plenty of time for revising and editing later. The point of the rough draft is to pull all of your ideas together and write all the fascinating things you have to say about your topic.

Sal's example

My original words:

I gave the lady beside me a high five.

In the margins of my paper, I found a lot more to say.
My expanded work:

In the wild excitement, I jumped right against the lady beside me. Oh no, I thought. She was cheering too, grinned and held out her palms. I gave her a high five. She was my grandmother's age.

Now I can go back to my organizer and check to see if this still fits as the last event of my story. If it doesn't, I can rework my organizer so my rough draft will flow better when I write it.

Ready-to-Go Writing Lessons That Teach Key Strategies
Scholastic Professional Books

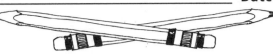

Your Turn

Go back to your freewriting and organizer (Lesson 9, *Making a Game Plan*, page 50) and find two or three places where you can expand your writing to tell more.

1. Original words:

_____

_____

Expanded work:

_____

_____

_____

_____

2. Original words:

_____

_____

Expanded work:

_____

_____

_____

_____

3. Original words:

_____

_____

Expanded work:

_____

_____

_____

_____

Ready-to-Go Writing Lessons That Teach Key Strategies
Scholastic Professional Books

Play the Game

Now you're ready for the rough-and-tumble of pulling your rough draft together. Here's my handy game plan for writing rough drafts. Make it yours, too!

Assemble and review your freewriting notes.

Establish a main idea for your draft and outline the structure on an organizer.

Insert words, phrases, and sentences to expand the freewriting and delete unnecessary parts.

Open with a "hook" to catch your reader.

Use your expanded freewriting, opening, and organizer to construct a rough draft.

As you write, encourage yourself until you're finished with all you want to say.

Writer _____

_____

_____

_____

_____

_____

_____

_____

_____

_____

_____

_____

_____

_____

_____

_____

Check It

Have you written all you need to say on this topic? Reread your piece and make sure that you've hit the parts listed in your organizer, that you've stuck to your main idea, and that you've added important details from your freewriting.

Ready-to-Go Writing Lessons That Teach Key Strategies
Scholastic Professional Books

Keeping the Ball in Play

Moving Past Writer's Block

Let's face it. Everyone who writes will hit writer's block at some point in the writing process and will wonder how to move beyond it. The answer does not lie in bumping up against the same old block again and again, but in applying strategies for working past the block. Suggestions in this lesson move students from panic and frustration into action and show them steps to start writing again.

Focus Students learn strategies to move beyond writer's block.

Writing links All writing.

Lesson activity, pages 62–64 While writing a rough draft of a personal essay, students learn three strategies to move beyond writer's block: reading the writing, asking questions, and freewriting.

Introducing the lesson Illustrate the principle of resistance by having students conduct an experiment. Ask students to line up with their left foot, left side, and left cheek to the wall. Then ask them to try to lift their right foot. Surprise! The rigid posture and balance will not allow them to do it. Only when they change their strategy by shifting their balance—moving away from the wall—are they able to lift the other foot. Tell students that writer's block requires the same kind of flexibility. They must be willing to change their strategy and shift their balance, so to speak.

Literature resource We've developed a strategy checklist called **SAFE** to help students push their writing beyond writer's block and begin writing again.

S Stop and reread what you have written.
When a writer gets lost, it's helpful to go back and find a familiar spot. Rereading the writing helps students get back on track.

A Ask questions.
An important tool for moving beyond the block is asking questions, such as the following:
What am I really writing about?
What do I really need to say about my topic?
What seems most interesting and important to me that I've already written?
Does my writing connect to my topic or the assignment?
Do I have enough material to write about the topic I've chosen?

F Freewrite on your answers to the questions.
It's not enough simply to answer the questions. The student needs to freewrite and expand on these answers to discover new thoughts on the topic.

E Energize your draft with these new ideas and direction.
Now it's time to take these fresh ideas back to the draft to infuse it with this new energy and direction.

TIP Writer's block is about resistance to the white page. But it does not always mean the writer has nothing to say. It can mean that the writer is wrestling with powerful emotions or thoughts. Your encouragement can demystify the problem and help to move the student through the block and back to the writing again. Begin by explaining that writer's block is a common experience among writers and by assuring your students that there are surefire ways to tackle this problem.

Keeping the Ball in Play

Moving Past Writer's Block

Listen Up: What do you do when you hit writer's block?

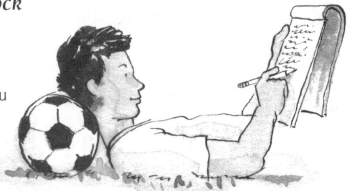

In spite of your best efforts, you may experience writer's block. It's like an opponent stepping right in front of you. You may feel frustrated and stuck.

We soccer players have a strategy for overcoming blocks. The call goes out to change our strategy, keep the ball in play, and get the game back on track. You can use the same idea in writing. When you hit a writer's block, don't sit there struggling and stalling. Play it SAFE and try a new move to keep your writing going.

When you face writer's block, what's one thing you do?

_____

_____

Practice

I began writing on the topic "My Number-One TV Show." But as I wrote, I didn't have a main idea and I hit a block. I stopped writing in frustration.

> **Sal's example**
>
> *As I flip on the TV, I surf the channels for the sports games, my favorite. I can always watch sports anytime—any day, any night. Last night, though, I stopped on the weather channel, and guess what? A storm was heading this way.*
>
> Oops! No wonder my writing stalled. I couldn't decide what I wanted to write about—the sports program or the weather channel. So I checked out my easy, effective strategy for moving my writing past a block—I call it SAFE!

First, I stopped and read my writing from the beginning. Next, I asked myself, *What am I really writing about?* That helped me know I was really trying to write

Ready-to-Go Writing Lessons That Teach Key Strategies
Scholastic Professional Books

about TV sports. (Maybe I'll decide to write about that storm some other time, but for now, I'm going to focus on TV sports.) Then I freewrote for more ideas on TV sports, and I energized my draft with my new ideas.

Your Turn

Now you freewrite on the topic "My Number-One TV Show" (or another topic of your choice).

_____

_____

_____

_____

_____

_____

_____

_____

_____

_____

> **Strategies to push past writer's block:**
>
> **S** Stop and reread.
>
> **A** Ask questions. *What am I really writing about? What do I really need to say about my topic? What seems most interesting and important to me that I've already written? Does my writing connect to my topic or the assignment? Do I have enough material to write about the topic I've chosen?*
>
> **F** Freewrite.
>
> **E** Energize your draft with new ideas.

Stop here! Imagine you've just hit a writing block. Follow the SAFE steps to see if you're on track or need to change the direction of your writing. Circle one of the following questions and give your answer to it below:

What am I really writing about?

What do I really need to say about my topic?

What seems most interesting and important to me that I've already written? Does my writing connect to my topic or the assignment?

Do I have enough material to write about the topic I've chosen?

_____

_____

_____

_____

_____

Ready-to-Go Writing Lessons That Teach Key Strategies
Scholastic Professional Books

 Play the Game

Write a rough draft of a personal essay titled "My Number-One TV Show." You can use your freewriting from **Your Turn** as a starting point, or you may choose to take a totally different direction. Remember, if you hit a block, refer to the SAFE steps.

My Number-One TV Show

or _____ (my topic)

_____

_____

_____

_____

_____

_____

_____

_____

_____

_____

_____

_____

_____

_____

_____

_____

_____

_____

S Stop and reread.

A Ask questions. *What am I really writing about? What do I really need to say about my topic? What seems most interesting and important to me that I've already written? Does my writing connect to my topic or the assignment? Do I have enough material to write about the topic I've chosen?*

F Freewrite.

E Energize your draft with new ideas.

 Check It

What worked best for you in the SAFE process? What advice would you give a friend who hit writer's block?

_____

_____

_____

_____

Cheers

Encouraging the Writer

Let's teach young writers to cheer on their writing. Let's encourage them to praise their writing, and only praise their writing, during the early steps. When the writing is just underway, criticism diminishes a writer's confidence, slows the writing (or stops it altogether), and stifles creativity. Students need to know how to motivate themselves and cheer their writing along. Wise teachers model praise by highlighting specific strong points in students' writing and teaching students to do the same.

Focus Students learn to praise and encourage their writing.

Writing links Personal narrative, poetry, short story, essays, and drama.

Lesson activity, pages 67–69 Students respond to prompts, write a paragraph, and create an imaginative story. Throughout the lesson they use motivational strategies to take risks in their writing and stretch their thinking.

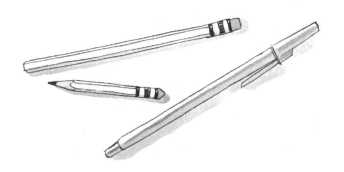

Introducing the lesson Have students gather in small groups and dig for the most divergent ideas and angles on writing topics through a word association game. Present the following (or your own) list of prompts:

ear	ice
volcano	happy
Oprah	basketball

Using these topics, encourage students to stretch for new and creative associations. Students can map out their ideas in a web format, simply list words, or freewrite.

Follow by asking students to share ideas from their brainstorming that surprised them. Cheer on these inventive responses and model the idea that we praise all our writing ideas, including divergent thinking. Writers should be especially supportive of their own work in the beginning stages and take care not to be too critical.

Literature resource In this excerpt from *Writing Down the Bones*, Natalie Goldberg writes about creating and editing one's writing.

It is important to separate the creator and editor or internal censor when you practice writing, so that the creator has free space to breathe, explore, and express. If the editor is absolutely annoying and you have trouble differentiating it from your creative voice, sit down whenever you need to and write what the editor is saying; give it full voice—"You are a jerk, whoever said you could write, I hate your work, I'm embarrassed, you have nothing valuable to say, and besides you can't spell. . . ." Sound familiar?

The more clearly you know the editor, the better you can ignore it. After a while, like the jabbering of an old . . . fool, it becomes just prattle in the background. Don't reinforce its power by listening to its empty words. If the voice says, "You are boring," and you listen to it and stop your hand from writing, that reinforces and gives credence to your editor. That voice knows that the term boring will stop you dead in your tracks, so you'll hear yourself saying that a lot about your writing. Hear "You are boring" as distant white laundry flapping in the breeze. Eventually it will dry up and someone miles away will fold it and take it in. Meanwhile you will continue to write.

TIP Have students try out these cheers—written or spoken—to move their writing along. It's important for students to give a reason for their comments so that they can practice identifying and internalizing their writing strengths (for example, *I like this opening because I used a shocking statement to grab my reader's attention*). Chances are, students who cheer themselves (and other writers) on like this will add many successful strategies to their repertoire.

Other examples:
You hooked me when you . . .
Tell me more about . . .
Strong word picture—I could really picture the
  part when . . .
Compelling action here!
I love the way that sentence . . .
Distinctive voice!
I hear you! I connected with this part because . . .
Impressive use of . . .
Wow! Strong verb!
Yes!
This part was poetic because . . .

Bright sticky notes are great tools for flagging good ideas right on the page without having to write on the actual draft.

Cheers

Encouraging the Writer

Listen Up: How do you stay motivated when you write?

"Great game!" "Way to go!" "Keep it up!" Cheers from the sidelines build my confidence, pump me up with energy, and inspire me to look for new moves on the field. The same cheers work for my writing, too, especially when I'm just beginning. But I can't always depend on cheers from others, either on the field or at my desk. I've learned to cheer for myself.

When I first start to write, I ignore all critical thoughts. They're like boos from the sidelines. If I choose to listen to them, they hurt my performance. Instead, I cheer on my writing and move forward, encouraging the flow of my pencil across the page, praising a new thought, recognizing the right word or phrase, or revealing my thoughts and feelings—just as I do when I run the ball down the field, cheering myself on toward the goal.

What's the best compliment you've ever received about your writing?

_____

_____

Remind yourself of it the next time you write!

Practice

The creative stage is the best time to praise your writing. I write comments on the page to cheer myself on in the writing, just as I cheer myself on in a game.

> **My Personal Cheers**
> *This works well because . . .*
> *Sounds great!*
> *This idea fits.*
> *Write more on this.*
> *My most powerful sentence!*
> *This surprised me!*
> *Something new.*
> *Hooks my reader!*

Sal's example

These setting details hook my reader!

The dark, endless tunnel of the hall stretched out before me and I strolled forward.

Ready-to-Go Writing Lessons That Teach Key Strategies
Scholastic Professional Books

Your Turn

Sketch out ideas for an imaginative story. Choose the topic below or come up with your own. And have no fear—just let the creative juices flow!

You're an alien who has crashed to Earth. You leave your battered spaceship and walk toward a large building. What happens?

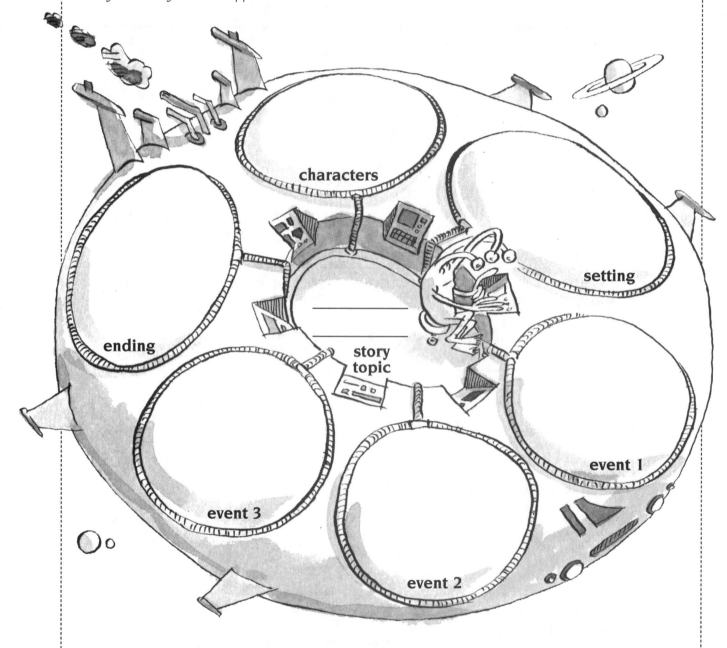

characters

setting

ending

story topic

event 1

event 3

event 2

Meet with a classmate. Star at least three of your favorite ideas for the imaginative story and write personal cheers around them.

Ready-to-Go Writing Lessons That Teach Key Strategies
Scholastic Professional Books

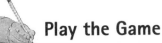

Play the Game

Write a rough draft of your story. Include specific details along with your thoughts and feelings about this strange new world or about your own topic choice.

_____
(title)

_____

_____

_____

_____

_____

_____

_____

_____

_____

_____

_____

_____

_____

_____

_____

_____

_____

_____

_____

_____

_____

✓ Check It

Jot some personal cheers on your own story. Then, share your draft with a classmate and talk about your positive reactions to each other's writing.

Check out your comments and your partner's comments. They might highlight strategies that you'll want to use again when you write.

Ready-to-Go Writing Lessons That Teach Key Strategies
Scholastic Professional Books

Strategic Moves

Revising the Writing

If there's one message on revision we teachers want to send to our students, it's that they need to become constructive critics of their own work: If they are invested in their writing, they will want to make comprehensive changes and revisions. But how can we teach students to revise or re-see a piece, to move the writing and its meaning forward? We help them first to appreciate the strengths of their writing—when they use a new word, construct a clear sentence, or add a fresh idea—thus building their confidence to jump into making their work even better (see Lesson 13: *Cheers, Encouraging the Writer*). Then we challenge them to look for areas in their writing that can use more attention—more or less detail, better structure, and so forth. Using constructive criticism, students can tackle the tough questions and go to work effectively on their revisions.

Focus Students learn to appreciate the strengths of their writing, identify areas for improvement, and then choose parts to revise.

Writing links All writing.

Lesson activity, pages 72–74 Students practice appreciating and then revising their own writing, working first on an excerpt from one of Sal's drafts and then on one of their own rough drafts. The Revision Checklist on page 74 serves as a guide for students to help them examine their own writing and that of their peers. The checklist guides them step by step according to many principles outlined in other lessons in this book. It does not, however, include every writing technique required for a strong writing piece. Feel free to add categories that will meet the needs of your students. The checklist is general enough to be adapted and used as a handy guide for revision.

Introducing the lesson Select a work of art by an abstract modernist such as Kandinsky, Miró, or Pollock—one unfamiliar to the students. Ask the class to list aspects of the artwork that they appreciate. Even if students do not "like" the artwork, encourage them to notice appealing details, such as color, lines, shapes, texture, angles, and other elements. Then ask them to define aspects of the work they might change and to explain why. This exercise calls for appreciating first and then critiquing, an order we want to emphasize.

Literature resource Revision is, to a large extent, a matter of personal choice. Different writers will find different areas to expand or to change structurally because each of us has a distinct way of seeing and re-seeing a piece. Present the sample paragraphs below to your class to stimulate a number of different responses and strategies for changes to strengthen the writing.

I wasn't excited about Uncle Martin's offer to my family—free tickets to Explorers' Park—and my mom wanted to know why. My younger sister was furious and Uncle Martin called back with all kinds of questions. So I finally said yes. He was a big airline pilot. I wasn't about to let him know I was a wimp. I didn't want him to think I was a baby who was afraid of heights.

For two years I had put off a trip to the park. Many times my mom encouraged the idea. I found excuses. "Wouldn't it be fun to take a friend to the park today?" she'd ask. I fussed about practicing flips on the trampoline, cleaning my aquarium or plans I already had made with my friends. Each time she frowned, not understanding why I wouldn't jump at the chance to experience the exciting action of the Alpine Twister. All my friends raved about it. I was the only one who

hadn't ridden it. But what she didn't know was that several years before, during a camping trip hike, I almost fell from the edge of a cliff when my foot slipped on a patch of leaves.

In revision, we look at all kinds of changes to strengthen the writing. Some of these include a more compelling opening, clear language, audience appeal, and stronger sentences. Notice the difference revision makes in the underlined changes below:

<u>So why wouldn't I want us to take up Uncle Martin's offer for free tickets to Explorers' Park?</u> That's what my mom wanted to know when I first replied, "No thanks." My younger sister was furious and Uncle Martin called back with all kinds of questions. So I finally said yes. <u>I wasn't about to let him, a big airline pilot, know I was a wimp, a baby who was afraid of heights.</u>

For two years I had put off a trip to the park. Many times my mom encouraged the idea. "Wouldn't it be fun to take a friend to the park today?" she'd ask. <u>Always I found excuses. I had to practice my flips on the trampoline. My aquarium needed cleaning. My friends and I already had planned "something."</u> Each time she frowned, not understanding why I wouldn't jump at the chance to experience the <u>gut-wrenching drops and turns of the Alpine Twister</u>. All my friends raved about it. I was the only one who hadn't ridden it. But what she didn't know was that several years before, during a camping trip hike, I almost fell from the edge of a cliff when my foot slipped on a patch of leaves.

Compelling opening

Beginning with a question rather than a statement creates more interest for the reader. The question represents the issue for the speaker, one that the other people in the speaker's life are asking.

Clear language

In the second paragraph, the writer fails to make a connection between "excuses" and the listed activities, but the revision clarifies the link.

Audience

A few changes in word choice reflect awareness of audience. In this case the writer targets an audience of peers—for example, changing *exciting* to *gut-wrenching* and *action* to *drops and turns*.

Strong sentences

Combining several short sentences at the end of the first paragraph creates a stronger and more cohesive sentence.

> **TIP** We want students to become active writers who coach themselves and make revision an integral part of their writing. Revising is an act of caring about their writing. We can inform students that professional writers are constantly rereading and revising their work. Jane Yolen said, "It's never perfect when I write it down the first time, or the second time, or the fifth time. But it always gets better as I go over it and over it."

Answers, page 73

Although **Your Turn** opens a wide range of possible responses, here are a few to consider:

Pelé, Brazil's star player, took his team to the top. Then in 1975, he joined the New York Cosmos. It was no surprise that the sport skyrocketed in popularity in the United States, too.

After taking Brazil's team to the top of the ladder, Pelé came to the United States in 1975 to play for the New York Cosmos. Then the sport took off in this country, too.

Pelé took Brazil's team to the top of the ladder before coming to the United States in 1975 to play for the New York Cosmos. And what do you think happened next? The sport took off in this country, too.

Ready-to-Go Writing Lessons That Teach Key Strategies
Scholastic Professional Books

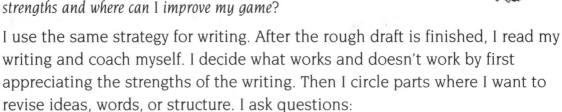

Strategic Moves

Revising the Writing

Listen Up: How do you revise?

The game of soccer has taught me to coach myself. As the referee blows the final whistle and I trot off the field, I ask myself, *How did I do? Did I follow my game plan? What are my strengths and where can I improve my game?*

I use the same strategy for writing. After the rough draft is finished, I read my writing and coach myself. I decide what works and doesn't work by first appreciating the strengths of the writing. Then I circle parts where I want to revise ideas, words, or structure. I ask questions:

Do I *have a compelling opening?*	Do I *use clear language?*
Who is my audience?	Do I *have strong sentences?*

When I come up with my own answers, I become my own writing coach.

Describe a time you coached and encouraged yourself, either in a game or on an assignment.

_____

_____

_____

_____

Practice

Here's an excerpt from the rough draft of a short biography.

Sal's example

Pelé may be the world's greatest soccer player. He started, joined Brazil's national team when he was sixteen and led them to championships in three separate years.

Now notice the changes with my revision.

Pelé, perhaps the world's greatest soccer player, joined Brazil's national team when he was sixteen and led them to championships in three separate years.

Ready-to-Go Writing Lessons That Teach Key Strategies
Scholastic Professional Books

Your Turn

Step into my cleats and pretend you're the writer revising the sentences below. Mark the parts you like and then make changes where needed.

Pelé took Brazil's team to the top of the ladder. He came to the United States in 1975. And played for the New York Cosmos. Then the sport took off in this country too.

> Revision includes changes I make to the word choice, style, and sentence and paragraph structure, but it does not include corrections for usage and the mechanics of writing, such as grammar, spelling, and punctuation. I save those for last.

_____

_____

_____

You can rework these words in a new way to offer a different sentence structure. Write a second revision of the sentences on Pelé.

_____

_____

_____

What differences do you see?

_____

_____

Play the Game

After writing, I coach myself with a tool called a Revision Checklist. It helps me evaluate my rough draft and make changes to improve my writing. Here's how you can use it to improve your writing:

First, choose a rough draft to revise. Then read through the checklist on the next page. You'll find familiar terms, skills, and strategies from other lessons. Use the checklist to check over and make important changes to your rough draft. Later, you can apply the Revision Checklist to a classmate's writing to help make changes.

 ## Check It

Partner with another reader and share your evaluation. Star two revisions that improved your writing the most.

Use this checklist as a game plan whenever you revise your rough drafts or anyone else's. Jump right onto the page and make your comments.

Revision Checklist

Name _____ Date _____

What do I appreciate about this writing?

☐ Star at least three improvements in the writing.

☐ Jot cheers in the margins.

What do I suggest for revision?

☐ After reading through the writing, can I identify the **main idea**? Underline one or two sentences that express this main idea. Then circle places in the writing that don't support this main idea. These are places to make changes or deletions.

☐ Who is the **audience** for this writing? _____
Identify content, descriptions, expressions, and words that match this audience.

☐ Label the paragraphs that mark the **opening**, **middle**, and **ending**. If the writing needs structure, which part needs the most work?

☐ Does the **opening** grab the reader's attention? (Yes/No) If yes, what strategy did the writer use: Amazing Action? Catchy Question? Dramatic Description? Surprising Statement? Or other? If no, what opening can the writer try?

☐ Identify places where the writer's **voice** is strong. Mark a V next to places where voice could be stronger.

☐ Star **sensory details** that enhance descriptions. Write *see, hear, taste, smell,* or *touch* next to areas to improve.

☐ Underline examples of **sentence variety** and **specific nouns and verbs**. Go back to the sentences or areas not underlined. Suggest ways the writer can play with the sentence structure, add clearer nouns, and insert active verbs.

☐ What **title** fits this writing? _____

Ready-to-Go Writing Lessons That Teach Key Strategies
Scholastic Professional Books

Fancy Footwork

Writing Strong Sentences

How can we cover "the sentence" in one easy lesson? We can't. Volumes are written on effective sentences. But we can alert students to the value of sentence variety in their writing. In fact, we know that the power of the entire work rests on the crafting and development of individual sentences. This lesson emphasizes how sentence variety can contribute to a strong, cohesive work.

Focus Students learn to vary sentences to strengthen their writing.

Writing links Personal narrative, short story, and essay.

Lesson activity, pages 76–78 Students learn the components of effective sentences, improve their own sentences in **Your Turn**, and combine sentences into a paragraph for an imaginative story or a personal essay.

Introducing the lesson Students will enjoy this example of strong sentences from the introductory paragraphs of *The Watsons Go to Birmingham—1963* by Christopher Paul Curtis.

It was one of those super-duper cold Saturdays. One of those days that when you breathed out your breath kind of hung in the air like a hunk of smoke and you could walk along and look exactly like a train blowing out big, fat, white puffs of smoke.

It was so cold that if you were stupid enough to go outside your eyes would automatically blink a thousand times all by themselves, probably so the juice inside of them wouldn't freeze up. It was so cold that if you spit, the slob would be an icecube before it hit the ground. It was about a zillion degrees below zero.

Call students' attention to characteristics of these strong sentences. First, the repetition of the beginning of the sentences focuses on that one extremely cold day. The second sentence is a sentence fragment, but it packs a descriptive, powerful punch. Finally, after several long sentences, the last sentence in the second paragraph succinctly sums it all up with a crisp hyperbole ("It was about a zillion degrees below zero.") and Curtis makes us feel that coldest-of-cold Michigan days.

Literature resource Some sentences are made more powerful when they are left simple. Ernest Hemingway's *The Old Man and the Sea* includes many sentences of a straightforward subject-predicate structure. Your students may enjoy hearing excerpts from this great American classic.

> **TIP** Often we believe we're doing students a service when we insist that they write in complete sentences all the time. However, we need to be careful not to prohibit the use of sentence fragments in students' writing work. Fragments frequently show up in excellent literature—especially fiction—for emphasis. Students need to be able to identify sentence fragments and use them effectively and purposefully in their own writing.

Ready-to-Go Writing Lessons That Teach Key Strategies
Scholastic Professional Books

Fancy Footwork
Writing Strong Sentences

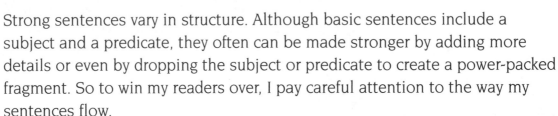

Listen Up: How do you develop strong sentences?

How do I score a goal and win the game? By combining my best moves as I take the ball down the field, dribbling, passing, and heading. The same goes for writing, where strong sentences are the fancy footwork for the game.

Strong sentences vary in structure. Although basic sentences include a subject and a predicate, they often can be made stronger by adding more details or even by dropping the subject or predicate to create a power-packed fragment. So to win my readers over, I pay careful attention to the way my sentences flow.

Practice

A basic sentence includes a subject and predicate. You can make it stronger by adding more details or joining other sentences or phrases to it.

> **Sal's example**
>
> *Joe is our star forward. Joe tripped over the backpack. He broke his leg.*
>
> These basic sentences are correct, but I can make them more powerful by combining them and adding more information.
>
> *While distracted by his friend in the hallway, Joe, our star forward, tripped over his backpack and broke his leg.*
>
> Occasionally authors use fragments to drive home an idea. Notice the fragment I added.
>
> *While distracted by his friend in the hallway, Joe, our star forward, tripped over his backpack and broke his leg. What a shock for the team!*

Ready-to-Go Writing Lessons That Teach Key Strategies
Scholastic Professional Books

Your Turn

Select a basic sentence from any of your writing and make it more powerful, just as I have in my examples above. Try combining ideas, adding more information, and maybe experimenting with a fragment.

My original sentence:

_____

My improved sentence(s):

_____

_____

_____

Play the Game

Write a paragraph with a variety of sentences on each of the topics below (or two topics of your choice). Your work will provide material for an imaginative short story or a personal essay.

For an imaginative story:

You're on a hike with a friend. Far up the mountainside you discover a dark opening, obviously to a cave, beside the path. Write a paragraph about what happens next.

_____

_____

_____

_____

_____

_____

_____

_____

_____

_____

_____

_____

Ready-to-Go Writing Lessons That Teach Key Strategies
Scholastic Professional Books

For a personal essay:

You travel into the future and become an author. What book would you write and why?

_____

_____

_____

_____

_____

_____

_____

_____

_____

_____

_____

_____

_____

_____

_____

_____

> Use the active voice—*Lisa drove the car*, not the passive voice—*The car was driven by Lisa.* When the subjects of your sentences (like Lisa!) perform the action, your sentences become stronger and your reader stays interested longer.

 Check It

In one paragraph above, underline impressive sentences that expand and combine ideas really well. Star sentences that pack a punch and write "frag" beside sentence fragments that work for you.

Ready-to-Go Writing Lessons That Teach Key Strategies
Scholastic Professional Books

Picture This

Finding the Right Nouns and Verbs

Do you ever wonder how to help student writers break the bad habit of using general, unclear, and vague nouns and verbs? You know the nouns we mean: *thing*, *chair*, *car*, or *plant*. You know the verbs we mean: *get*, *like*, *put*, *walk*, *make*, and many forms of the verb *to be*. This lesson coaches students in the skill of kicking out imprecise words and kicking in exact, descriptive language to paint a clear picture for the reader. Student writers learn to express and entertain, just as the writing masters have been doing for ages.

Focus Students learn to select exact nouns and verbs to give the reader a clear word picture.

Writing links Poetry, short story, and essay.

Lesson activity, pages 80–82 Students find their own specific nouns and verbs, write sentences, and craft a descriptive narrative about creating a clever costume.

Introducing the lesson Students can recognize the value of more precise nouns and verbs by keeping a list of the words they can substitute for tired words like the noun *food* and the verb *say*. Begin classroom lists on chart paper for each word your class has chosen and challenge students to make each list grow and grow over several weeks. Your walls will become a terrific writing resource!

Literature resource The following excerpt from *Watership Down* by Richard Adams illustrates the value of using well-chosen nouns and verbs. Point out to students that some words remain general, but Adams includes clear, descriptive words where they have the greatest impact. In this action-filled passage, three rabbits encounter and fend off a threatening crow.

Hazel covered the distance down the slope in a few seconds. He had no idea what he was going to do, and if the crow had ignored him he would probably have been at a loss. But by dashing up he distracted its attention and it turned on him. He swerved past it, stopped and, looking back, saw Bigwig come racing in from the opposite side. The crow turned again, struck at Bigwig and missed. Hazel heard its beak hit a pebble in the grass with a sound like a snail shell when a thrush beats it on a stone. As Silver followed Bigwig, it recovered itself and faced him squarely. Silver stopped short in fear and the crow seemed to dance before him, its great black wings flapping in a horrible commotion. It was just about to stab when Bigwig ran straight into it from behind and knocked it sideways, so that it staggered across the turf with a harsh, raucous cawing of rage.

TIP Reward your students when they use a new specific noun or verb. Keep a list of the most interesting words you see in their writing. Choose several each week and make them the class words of the week. Write these words on the board and challenge yourself and your students to use them in speaking and in writing until they become a natural part of everyone's vocabulary.

Ready-to-Go Writing Lessons That Teach Key Strategies
Scholastic Professional Books

Picture This

Finding the Right Nouns and Verbs

Listen Up: What nouns and verbs create a clear word picture?

When I'm on the field, I need to use precise words. As team captain, I can't say "things" when I mean "cleats." I can't say "move the ball" when I mean "pass." My team wouldn't know what to do.

It's equally important for me when I'm writing to find exactly the right words for my reader. Like any other good writer, I want to give the most complete picture possible because I want my reader to see what I see.

Fuzzy and vague verbs tell your reader nothing about the action. Instead of *see*, the reader needs *stare, gaze, peek,* or *glance*. If a writer refers to *tree*, is that noun clear enough? Does the reader see the tree the writer saw, or should the writer use a more specific noun, such as *dogwood, maple,* or *oak,* and an adjective such as *barren,* or *blossoming,* or *ancient*? Write with this thought in mind: Readers can see only as much as we writers show them.

> Mark Twain said it best: "The difference between the almost right word & the right word is really a large matter—it's the difference between the lightning bug & the lightning."
>
> (from a letter to George Bainton, October 15, 1888)

Practice

It's time to find your own specific nouns and verbs. Let this example warm up your writing muscles.

Sal's example

general noun	**specific**	**more specific**	**most specific**
furniture	chair	rocking chair	antique rocker

general verb	**specific**	**more specific**	**most specific**
move	run	race	charge

Ready-to-Go Writing Lessons That Teach Key Strategies
Scholastic Professional Books

Name _____ Date _____

Your Turn

Fill in the chart with nouns and verbs that are as specific as possible.

general noun	specific	more specific	most specific
dog	purebred	_____	_____
flower	_____	_____	_____
gift	_____	_____	_____

general verb	specific	more specific	most specific
move	_____	_____	_____
get	_____	_____	_____
walk	_____	_____	_____

For more practice, take the word **say** and find eight specific verbs to replace it.

 _____    _____

 _____    _____

 _____    _____

 _____    _____

Now write a descriptive sentence using your most specific noun from the list and then a sentence using your most specific verb from the list.

1. _____

_____

_____

_____

2. _____

_____

_____

_____

Ready-to-Go Writing Lessons That Teach Key Strategies
Scholastic Professional Books

Play the Game

Write a descriptive paragraph explaining how to make a clever costume.
Entertain your reader. Use powerful sentences with clear nouns and strong
verbs. Write so your reader can see every step.

How to Make _____

_____
(opening)

_____

_____

First, _____

_____

_____

_____

Second, _____

_____

_____

_____

Third, _____

_____

_____

_____

Finally, _____

_____

_____

_____

 ## Check It

Circle any boring nouns and verbs that don't paint a picture for your reader.
Substitute new, exact words for these weak nouns and verbs. See if you can
use any of the specific nouns or verbs you collected in **Your Turn** on page 81.

Playing by the Rules

Editing to Make It Right

Too often student writers depend on someone else to fix their mistakes when, in fact, editing is their own responsibility. The idea here is to expand students' responsibility by extending their understanding of the editing stage in the writing process. This lesson introduces the whys and the hows of editing. The why is easy: Writers edit their work because they care about their final product and also realize that their readers deserve, respect, and expect clear, unhindered writing. The how—as always—is more complex, and this lesson introduces the process and some basic tools students need.

Focus Students learn the role of editing in the writing process.

Writing links All writing.

Lesson activity, pages 84–86 Students compare edited and unedited sentences and then use an editing rubric to polish a piece of their writing.

Introducing the lesson Remind students of the common errors in grammar, spelling, and punctuation by asking them what mistakes they notice most frequently in their writing. You can begin with a few mistakes our students have noticed in their writing:

- Confusion about it's/its; too/to/two; you're/your; they're/their.

- Subject-verb agreement with interrupting phrases. (For example: Each pencil in the boxes *have* already been sharpened. *Has* is the correct verb form.)

- Run-on sentences using commas in place of periods. (For example: *She ran for miles, she stopped short suddenly.* These sentences should be separated with a period or joined with a semicolon or coordinating conjunction.)

Literature resource

Be sure to have age-appropriate resources on hand for your students as they edit. We suggest the following titles:

Punctuation Power by Marvin Terban. Grades 4–8

Scholastic Children's Thesaurus by John K. Bollard. Grades 4–8

The Scholastic Dictionary of Spelling by Marvin Terban. Grades 5 and up

Writing with Style by Sue Young. Grades 5 and up

> **TIP** Now, after the creative stage, is the best time in the writing process to focus on editing. Students are truly invested in their work and are more willing to make improvements and changes. You can help students take responsibility for identifying and fixing their own mistakes by having them generate individual or group reference booklets for editing, such as an alphabetized "Troublesome Words" list, a "Worst Sentences Ever" book full of examples of grammatical errors to avoid, or a "Perfect Punctuation" sheet with example sentences corrected for common punctuation mistakes.

Answers to **Your Turn**, page 85:

Alfonso sat on the porch trying to push his crooked teeth to where he thought they belonged. He hated the way he looked. Last week he did a hundred sit-ups a day, thinking that he would burn those already apparent ripples on his stomach to even deeper ripples, dark ones, so when he went swimming at the canal next summer, girls in cutoffs would notice. (from "Growing Pains" by Gary Soto)

Playing by the Rules

Editing to Make It Right

Listen Up: How and why do you edit?

In a soccer game, we play by the rules. When we slip up, the referee blows the whistle and reminds us to play in an orderly way. Writing has its set of rules and regulations, too. This lesson blows the whistle to remind you it's time to apply them. For writers, this work of checking and correcting usage, spelling, and punctuation is called *editing*.

Writers edit because good writing that follows the rules is easier—and more enjoyable—to read. Readers respect writing that is correct. What's more, they expect it. What's even more, they deserve it. When your writing follows the rules of editing, you'll win over readers.

What is one common error you make in spelling, punctuation, or grammar when you write?

_____

_____

_____

> Your expert tools for editing are a comprehensive dictionary, a reliable thesaurus, and a handbook on usage and punctuation that you feel comfortable using.

Practice

Now let's look more closely at strategies for editing. When I'm writing, I always have a tough time with run-on sentences, subject-verb agreement, and the words *to* and *too*. So when I'm ready to edit, I keep a close eye on these. Here's a sentence from my narrative, "On the Sidelines," that shows you what I mean.

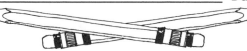

Sal's example

The players on the bench and the team manager was eating oranges during the S-V

first half, the coach was eating his share, to. SP.

See how the Editing Rubric helps me make corrections:

The players on the bench and the team manager were eating oranges during the first half. The coach was eating his share, too.

See what a difference it makes to split up separate sentences, make the subject and verb agree, correct the spelling of *to*, and add a comma before *too*?

Your Turn

Practice your editing skills and clean up a paragraph from a draft of your own writing or work on the paragraph below, an excerpt from Gary Soto's story "Growing Pains." Check carefully for spelling, punctuation, and usage mistakes.

alfonso set on the porch trying to push his crooked teeth too where he

thought they belonged. He hated the way he looked. Last week, he did a

hundred sit-ups a day, thinking that he would burn those already apperent

rippels, on his stomach to even deeper ripples, dark ones, so when he

went swimming at the canal next summer, girls' in cutoffs would notice.

Play the Game

Practice editing your work. Select any rough draft of your writing (for example, your rough draft from Lesson 11, *Pulling Your Game Together*) and use the Editing Rubric on page 86. Mark your corrections on the draft.

✓ Check It

When you've finished, ask a partner to edit your work for anything your eyes have missed. You can do the same for your partner's draft.

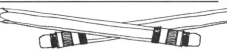

Editing Rubric

Editing Marks

Ap.◯

Spelling

☐ Have I spelled every word correctly? (Circle words to check.)

b̲ (capitalize)

B̸ (set lower case)

Capitalization

☐ Have I capitalized proper names, the first word in every sentence, and the first word in each quotation?

⊙ ?̂ !̂

Punctuation

☐ Have I used end marks (periods, question marks, and exclamation points) to punctuate each sentence correctly?

↢

☐ Have I used commas correctly (between items in a series, after introductory words and phrases, with dates and places, and with quotations)?

ᵛ̈ ᵛ̈

☐ If I've used dialogue, are my quotation marks placed at the beginning and at the end of the speaker's words, and have I made a new paragraph for each speaker?

Verbs

☐ Did I use the active voice (I *wrote the story*; not *The story was written by me*)?

S-V

☐ Did I check each sentence for subject-verb agreement?

☐ Did I pick a tense (past or present) and stay with it?

∧ (insert)

Sentences

☐ Have I checked for run-on sentences and unwanted fragments?

𝓮 (delete)

☐ Have I inserted all necessary words and deleted all unnecessary words?

¶

Paragraphs

☐ Have I indented each new paragraph?

☐ Have I developed my main idea (focus) with each new paragraph?

Ready-to-Go Writing Lessons That Teach Key Strategies
Scholastic Professional Books

Player Profile

Assessing Writing Progress

Are young writers ready to assess their own writing progress? You bet! At this stage, they're evaluating many other facets of their lives—dress, food, music, friends, etc.—and they are ready, willing, and able to take on the larger view of their writing progress, too. Like all of us, they benefit from others' responses but need to learn skills to evaluate their writing so they don't depend solely on others' critiques. It is this personal awareness of skills and progress that allows the most growth and increases confidence in writing.

Focus Students learn to assess their writing progress over time.

Writing links All writing.

Lesson activity, pages 89–91 Students review their collection of writing in preparation for drafting a reflective letter on their progress.

Introducing the lesson Ask students to identify a sentence from their writing that they like, briefly explain what they like about it, and read it to the class. Urge them to be specific. Share the reflective letter sample by student Laura Grabau on page 88 with students before they write their own reflective letters in **Play the Game**.

Literature resource In her book *In the Middle*, writing teacher Nancie Atwell shares her surprise at students' reflective comments on what they have learned:

Just recently I asked each eighth grader, "What's the most important or useful thing you learned as a writer during this first quarter of writing workshop?" What I

thought they would give back to me is what I thought I had given them. I thought I had stressed leads and conclusions, self-editing, and a writer's need to be her own first critic—things I thought the whole class needed to know. Instead, in one class students named over thirty different areas of growth, from specific skills (. . . "probably the thing about not connecting sentences with a comma," . . .) to specific writing techniques (. . . "different kinds of leads" . . .) to general writing concerns ("looking at my writing from a reader's point of view" . . .).

TIP The end of the marking period or curriculum unit is a good time for students to assess their writing progress and set new goals. A thorough, reflective letter helps this process, and questions are the best guide for the letter. Encourage students to give specific examples from their work to support their answers.

How has writing opened your eyes to the world around you?

How have you grown as a writer?

What is your favorite piece? Why?

What are the most helpful strategies you use when you organize, draft, revise, and edit?

What is a new revision step you use?

What are you learning from reading other writers' works?

What are your writing goals for next year? For five years from now?

Ready-to-Go Writing Lessons That Teach Key Strategies
Scholastic Professional Books

Reflective Letter

Dear Reviewer,

How do you make a plant, such as a flower grow? Well, you water it and you make sure it has enough sunlight and is in a good environment. I find that my writing is similar to a blossoming flower in that it grows and matures as time passes. I must water it and take care of it, though, for it to become a beautiful flower.

There are many ways in which I have strengthened and grown as a writer in the past few years. I have developed rich and descriptive language that will help readers feel more a part of the story. This comes in part from reading a variety of books. I pick up on new words in the books I read and adapt them into my own writing. Several of my favorite authors are L. M. Montgomery, Brian Jacques, John Ende, and J. K. Rowling. Their books are excellent examples of what I hope my writing will be someday.

I have also begun to use more of a variety of sentence structures. . . . Sentences, or maybe even words are like seeds of my flower. They are the beginning of every story, poem, or article. I have also used more detailed sentences. Details are one thing I struggle with because sometimes it's hard to tell if I need more, or if I'm carrying an overload. . . .

My strongest piece is probably my literary piece, entitled "The Coin Boy." I think I have managed to convey some strong feelings and settings in it, and it hopefully has an appropriate amount of details in it. I originally had some very confusing ideas and transitions, but after peer/teacher revising and editing, I deleted them or changed them to fit the scene and characters better.

The approaches I used to compose my writing portfolio pieces were varied. I used ideas that were fairly familiar to me. For example, in my personal essay about poverty I wrote about something I knew about, poverty. I also used more freewriting and brainstorming to come up with ideas to use. This proved an effective method and two of my four pieces begin with it. . . .

. . . Writing takes a lot of time and effort; it's not an overnight process. I have carefully selected pieces that show my writing talent. . . . I have worked toward establishing a better purpose and audience. I have used more appropriate details and more rich language. I have improved tremendously this year, and in the future I plan to become the most beautiful flower possible. . . . and to learn even more about how to grow stronger as a budding writer.

Sincerely,
Laura Grabau
Winburn Middle School

Name _____ Date _____

Player Profile
Assessing Writing Progress

Listen Up: Notice any progress? How have you changed and grown as a writer?

After our game the local sports reporter interviews the players and asks questions. "How has your game changed since last season?" "What are your game strengths now?" and "What do you see for the future?" are some of her favorites. The answers to these questions help me create my own player profile.

You can develop a writer profile, too, by paying attention to what you've learned about writing and how your writing changes over time. Don't wait around for grades or teacher comments to tell you how your writing's going. You are your best critic. You know what it feels like to play the entire game: the sweat of hard work, the sweetness of triumph.

Ask yourself: *What have I learned about writing? What am I doing to improve my writing? What do I wish I knew about writing?* Put your answers to these and other questions in a reflective letter and you will have your writer profile. I bet you'll be amazed by how much your writing game has developed.

Name one improvement you've made in your writing.

_____

_____

Practice

Last year on the soccer field I had three assists, and this year I had seven. So now I can look back and see improvement. The same is true with my writing.

Sal's example

A year ago I hated the blank page. Every writing assignment left me sweating. Now I use freewriting to move my writing ideas onto the page. With freewriting, the blank page isn't so scary anymore. I also handed in all of my assignments this year, a big achievement for me.

Ready-to-Go Writing Lessons That Teach Key Strategies
Scholastic Professional Books

Your Turn

Go back and look through your collection of writing to generate some ideas about your progress. List three to six areas of your writing where you've improved.

- _____
  _____
- _____
  _____
- _____
  _____
- _____
  _____
- _____
  _____
- _____
  _____

Play the Game

Writing a reflective letter trains you to develop and grow as a writer. Here's how to start.

Select three areas of improvement listed under **Your Turn** and give examples of each from your writing. Use these to write a reflective letter discussing the writing skills and knowledge you have learned. Your audience may be the reviewer of your portfolio, your teacher, peers, parents, or yourself. End with your future goals for writing—the improvements you want to accomplish in the writing assignments ahead. You'll be proud of your progress.

> These questions may help you think about the ways you've grown as a writer:
>
> *How has writing opened your eyes to the world around you?*
> *How have you grown as a writer?*
> *What is your favorite piece? Why?*
> *What helpful strategies do you use to organize, draft, revise, and edit?*
> *What is a new revision step you use?*
> *What are you learning from reading other writers' works?*
> *What are your writing goals for next year? For five years from now?*

Ready-to-Go Writing Lessons That Teach Key Strategies
Scholastic Professional Books

Name _____ Date _____

Dear _____ (Reader),

_____
_____
_____
_____
_____
_____
_____
_____
_____
_____
_____
_____
_____
_____
_____
_____
_____
_____
_____
_____
_____

_____ (your name)

✓ **Check It**

How did the reflective letter help you understand your accomplishments and set new goals as a writer?

_____
_____

Ready-to-Go Writing Lessons That Teach Key Strategies
Scholastic Professional Books

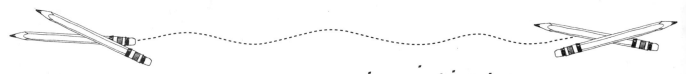

Celebrating the Game

Presenting and Publishing

Teachers know that meaningful writing needs to be shared and celebrated in the classroom. Although classroom writing does not generally earn trophies or big awards, you and your students can create ways to share finished work with an audience. Here are some ways to provide opportunities for students to share their work and to recognize their writing as achievements and contributions to the literary world of your classroom. Who knows where it will go from there?

Oral Presentations As a teacher, you can use many venues for helping students to share their writing. Frequently model an effective reading by choosing published poems or excerpts (and ones you've written, too). This will set a standard for student sharing. Here's how to do it.

✳ Introduce the piece by giving your name and the title of what you are reading.

✳ Demonstrate reading with clarity and expression.

✳ At the end of the reading, invite students to discuss the aspects of the reading that helped or hindered their enjoyment. (The Guidelines for Oral Presentation on page 93 support this assessment.)

Another way students can learn about effective oral presentations is to check out audio books of well-known writers reading their works. There are hundreds available, including J. R. R. Tolkien's recordings of *The Hobbit* and *The Lord of the Rings* series and Maya Angelou's *I Know Why the Caged Bird Sings*. Students will be surprised at the impact of hearing the familiar words come alive in the writer's voice.

Other Types of Presentations There are many other ways to celebrate student writing, and these are especially effective for students who are uncomfortable presenting in front of a large audience.

✳ Organize students in partnerships or groups of three. Have them read their pieces aloud and then provide one another with extensive oral comments and suggestions.

✳ Compile an anthology of classroom writing to which each student contributes a special piece. The anthology may consist of mixed genres or focus on a single genre, such as personal narratives.

✳ Conduct a "museum celebration"—a viewing of students' work—and allow guest readers to browse silently and enjoy the writing on display. Readers provide written feedback on each piece. This kind of celebration can be done within a single class or by invitation to outside guests: another class, parents, or local writers.

✳ Introduce students to Internet sites that may publish their writing.
 CRUNCH
 HYPERLINK http://nces.ed.gov/nceskids/crunch

 English Online Writer's Window
 HYPERLINK http://english.unitecnology.ac.nz/writers/home.html

 ZOOM: Send It To Zoom
 HYPERLINK http://www.pbs.org/wgbh/zoom/sendit/

Ready-to-Go Writing Lessons That Teach Key Strategies
Scholastic Professional Books

Guidelines for Oral Presentation

It's on-the-field time! Use the checklist below to make sure you're ready to share your writing with your fans.

Introducing Your Writing

The "intro" is short and personal but essential to setting the stage for your reading. Your fans will want to know what motivated you to write your piece and what your experience was like along the way. Here are some pointers to check off one by one:

☐ Make eye contact with the audience.

☐ Include my own name.

☐ Include the title of my work.

☐ Include comments on the writing:
      what I enjoyed, what I learned, where I found inspiration.

☐ _____
(Any other pointers I want to include.)

Reading Your Writing

When it's time to present, remember first the word "practice." Read before a mirror, read to your family, read to the family dog!—anything to become familiar with speaking your words. Here are the guidelines:

☐ Speak clearly in an audible voice.

☐ Read with expression (the emotion and meaning the writer intended).

☐ Make eye contact with the audience.

Good Game!

Ready-to-Go Writing Lessons That Teach Key Strategies
Scholastic Professional Books

Scheduling the Games

Keeping a Record

These pages may help you keep a record of the writing skills taught in your language arts curriculum. You may note the date and make comments.

Teacher _____ Class _____ Year _____

WARM UP

Lesson 1   The Familiar Field/Finding Writing Material   Date completed _____

_____

_____

Lesson 2   Kicking the Ball Around/Freewriting to Loosen Up   Date completed _____

_____

_____

Lesson 3   Describing the Plays/Using Sensory Details   Date completed _____

_____

_____

Lesson 4   Reading up on the Game/Learning from Other Writers   Date completed _____

_____

_____

PRACTICE

Lesson 5   Your Own Playing Style/Finding the Writer's Voice   Date completed _____

_____

_____

Lesson 6   Team Talk/Capturing Dialogue   Date completed _____

_____

_____

Lesson 7   The Game from Inside/Revealing the Writer's Thoughts and Feelings   Date completed _____

_____

_____

Lesson 8   Spectators and Fans/Writing for an Audience   Date completed _____

_____

_____

ON THE FIELD

Lesson 9   Making a Game Plan/Organizing the Writing   Date completed _____

_____

_____

Ready-to-Go Writing Lessons That Teach Key Strategies
Scholastic Professional Books

ON THE SIDELINES

CELEBRATING THE GAME

Comments _____

_____

_____

_____

_____

_____

Ready-to-Go Writing Lessons That Teach Key Strategies
Scholastic Professional Books

Bibliography

Student Reference Texts

Bollard, John K. *Scholastic Children's Thesaurus*. New York: Scholastic, 1998.

Terban, Marvin. *Punctuation Power*. New York: Scholastic, 2000.

_____. *The Scholastic Dictionary of Spelling*. New York: Scholastic, 2000.

Young, Sue. *Writing with Style*. New York: Scholastic, 1997.

Teacher Resources

Atwell, Nancie. *In the Middle: Writing, Reading, and Learning with Adolescents*. Portsmouth, NH: Heinemann, 1987.

Goldberg, Natalie. *Writing Down the Bones: Feeling the Writer Within*. Boston: Shambhala, 1986.

McQuade, Donald, and Robert Atwan, eds. *The Writer's Presence*. New York: St. Martin's Press, 2000.

Murray, Donald. *The Craft of Revision*. 3rd ed. Orlando, FL: Harcourt, 1997.

Ray, Katie. *Wondrous Words*. Urbana, IL: NCTE, 1999.

Literature Resources

Adams, Richard. *Watership Down*. New York: Avon, 1972.

Bolger, Francis W. P., and Elizabeth R. Epperly, eds. *My Dear Mr. M.: Letters to G. B. MacMillan from L. M. Montgomery*. CITY: McGraw-Hill Ryerson, 1980.

Bryson, Bill. *A Walk in the Woods*. New York: Broadway Books, 1999.

Cisneros, Sandra. "Eleven." *Woman Hollering Creek and Other Stories*. New York: Random House, 1991.

Cormier, Robert. *The Chocolate War*. New York: Dell Publishing, 1986.

Curtis, Christopher Paul. *The Watsons Go to Birmingham—1963*. New York: Bantam Books, 1997.

Didion, Joan. "On Keeping a Notebook." *Slouching Towards Bethlehem*. New York: Farrar, Straus & Giroux, 1968.

Hemingway, Ernest. *The Old Man and the Sea*. New York: Simon & Schuster Inc., 1995.

Hughes, Langston. "Subway Rush Hour." *Collected Poems*, edited by Arnold Rampersad. New York: Knopf, 1994.

Hughes, Ted. "The Thought-Fox." *Selected Poems, 1957–1967*. New York: Harper, 1974.

Konigsburg, E. L. *From the Mixed-up Files of Mrs. Basil E. Frankweiler*. New York: Atheneum, 1976.

Montgomery, L. M. *Anne of Avonlea*. New York: Bantam Books, 1987.

Nightengale, Earl. "Sparky." *Chicken Soup for the Teenage Soul*, edited by Jack Canfield et al. Deerfield Beach, FL: Health Communications, 1997.

Pendergraft, Patricia. "Miracle at Clement's Pond." In Trelease, *Read All About It*.

Rasmussen, R. Kent. *The Quotable Mark Twain*. Illinois: Contemprary Books, 1997.

Rawls, Wilson. *Where the Red Fern Grows*. New York: Bantam Books, 1988.

Robinson, Barbara, *The Best Christmas Pageant Ever*. In *Plays Children Love*. Vol. II. Edited by Coleman A. Jennings and Aurand Harris. New York: St. Martin's Press, 1988.

Simon, Neil. *Lost in Yonkers*. New York: Random House, 1992.

Soto, Gary. "Growing Pains." In Trelease, *Read All About It*.

Strasberg, Andy, as told to Mike Bryan. "The Andy Strasberg Story." In Trelease, *Read All About It*.

Tolkien, J. R. R. *The Hobbit: Or There and Back Again*. Boston: Houghton Mifflin, 1984.

Trelease, Jim, ed. *Read All About It*. New York: Penguin, 1993.

Wilder, Laura Ingalls. *Little House on the Prairie*. New York: Harper, 1935.

Ready-to-Go Writing Lessons That Teach Key Strategies
Scholastic Professional Books